THE POWER OF PROPHECY:

IT'S IN THE WORD

Understanding the Realm of the Spirit

E. BERNARD JORDAN

FOGHORN
PUBLISHERS

"Of Making Many Books There Is No End. . ."

THE POWER OF PROPHECY:

IT'S IN THE WORD

Understanding the Realm of the Spirit

The Power of Prophecy: It's In The Word - Understanding the Realm of the Spirit

Zoe Ministries
310 Riverside Drive
New York, NY 10025
(212)-316-2177
(212) 316-5769 – fax

ISBN: 0-9779452-4-3
Printed in the United States of America

Foghorn Publishers
P.O. Box 8286
Manchester, CT 06040-0286
860-216-5622
860-290-8291 fax.
foghornpublisher@aol.com

1 2 3 4 5 6 7 8 9 10 / 09 08 07 06

TABLE OF CONTENTS

PREFACE

"The moment you discover who He is, you will discover who YOU are!"

—Bishop E. Bernard Jordan

Whose report will you believe? Will you believe the report of man, your circumstances in life, or the obstacles that may seemingly be in your way? Will you believe the report of the doctor, the mortgage lender, the bill collector, or your child's teacher? Will you believe the report of the government, the school system, or the judicial system? Or will you believe that God is all in all? In this hour, God is sounding the alarm for His prophets to come forth and declare His report. For His report supersedes man's report. His report is the end all and be all. So whose report will you believe? For you are a part of a prophetic generation.

The prophet is the voice of God in the earth called to bring man back into right relationship with Him. God uses the prophet to bring direction, clarity, and definition to His people. God uses the prophet to call forth those dreams, giftings, and talents that often lie dormant within man. God wants His people to walk in Divine Oneness with Him, and He desires for His people to begin to recognize and understand who they are in Him.

God is raising up prophets who will proclaim His name in the earth. He is using the prophets to speak to nations, kingdoms, heads of state, and governmental institutions in society. God is using His prophets to bring change in the world and to the area in which they are assigned. God is calling for His prophets to move in the center of their expertise and redesign their environment. Whether it's in business, government, arts, music, or the Church, God wants His prophets to become models of His Word, to walk in His Divine Nature, and to operate according to His Divine Favor.

God has ordained you to be a winner in life. However, if you don't have the spirit of a winner, you will never succeed in life. If you don't have the mindset and the attitude that you are victorious, you will not be an overcomer. In this hour, God is bringing forth His prophets to reshape the mind of man and to change the thoughts of His people. He wants to destroy some of the "sacred cows" that His people have so diligently upheld in their lives, and thus have only worked toward their demise. But growth demands change! Change of values, beliefs, opinions and, what Rev. Ike describes as "stinking thinking." There is no devil outside of you causing havoc in your life. No! You must change your belief system. Stop believing the lies that the world has woven into the very fabric of your thinking.

For God says, "you are victorious!" "You are the head and not the tail, above only and not beneath." (Deuteronomy 28:13) L.S. Hamaker once said, *"Always remember that the soundest way to progress in any organization is to help the person ahead of you to get promoted."* Beloved, it is my desire that you get promoted to the next level of life. It is my desire to bring you into a level of mastery over the vicissitudes of life and teach you how to walk in your Divine Sonship. It is my desire that you receive <u>ALL</u> that God has earmarked for you to enjoy while dwelling here on earth!

By understanding and applying the principles outlined in the next pages, and taking hold of the mystery that "It is In The Word!" God is going to begin to reshape your world right before your very eyes. Get ready, because God is going to elevate you to the next level in Him!

INTRODUCTION

There are five kingdoms of life: the mineral kingdom, the vegetable kingdom, the animal kingdom, man's kingdom, and the Kingdom of God. Each kingdom expresses a degree of intelligence, the unfolding of which is expressed in many forms. However, the ultimate kingdom is the kingdom of God, where Divine Intelligence is expressed in the fullness. The truths that are vital to survival in the earth realm can be found in the kingdom of God. The prophet is able to unlock the truths and the mysteries that are resident in the mind of God so that the people of God can live a life of wholeness and completeness in mind, body and spirit. Therefore, the prophet must embrace the Age that he is in, as well as embrace science, in order to be effective in this Age and universal in his approach. The power is in the Prophetic Word! That is the Power of Prophecy!

In the following pages we will discover the mysteries of the kingdom and unveil the universal truths that will move people into the next dimension of God, as we realize that everything has its beginning in you, whether it is good, bad, or indifferent. You will gain a better understanding of the darkness, and discover that there are things trapped in the darkness waiting for you to declare, "Let there be." Darkness is just a place of unformed purpose. You will discover the power of letting others into your world of creation in order to experience the harvest. That is the Power of Prophecy!

As we learn how to go within our chemistry lab (our temple), to do the prophetic work of handling the mysteries of God and turning thoughts into things by shifting things with our eyes, we are able to change that which is base into that which is valuable in the twinkling of an eye. Despite any challenges, the prophet realizes that the ability to do this work is vital to saving the tribe. This will prepare us for the coming age of knowing God and will cause the way of the prophetic alchemist to have global impact.

For there is a world behind your eyes that is greater than that which is in front of your eyes. You have to be aware of this world in order to manifest your supply. Your supply will come from something that is already in your hands. Therefore, you must take inventory of what is in your house. We find that God takes pleasure in your prosperity and desires that you become a multiplier. However, you must be obedient and follow the instructions regarding your seed. You must make sure that your seed is planted in the right place. In the wrong environment, your seed becomes a weed, but in the right environment it will produce a harvest. The prophet has the uncanny ability to recognize the invisible supply within you, and also, those in the presence of the

Prophet must discern the invisible supply in their midst. That is the Power of Prophecy!

The Power of Prophecy will reshape your understanding of the role of the prophet in the earth. The prophet declares the word of the Lord. The prophet declares the mind of God. When the prophet gives a prophetic word, heaven hears. When the prophet speaks, the earth responds. Those who come to the prophet come to see the one through whom God has manifested Himself. Therefore, those who come before the prophet should never come empty-handed, but should always come with a seed. Those who sow a seed will receive from God the prophet's reward. For the Bible says, *"Surely the Lord God will do nothing, but he revealeth his secret unto His servants the prophets."* (Amos. 3:7)

God is the beginning of everything. God is all in all. We are made in the image of God. Therefore, we must demonstrate God. We must demonstrate the "Many Breasted One." This will provide us the balance that we need to resist duality in our thinking, to seek out darkness and get to our unformed purposes, and to generate our harvest in the midst of a void over and over again. That is the Power of Prophecy! It's in the Word!

CHAPTER 1

FINDING YOUR PROPHETIC VOICE

—⊫✦⊨—

"The universe is a mirror of who YOU are!"
—Bishop E. Bernard Jordan

In The Beginning God...

"In the beginning God created the heavens and the earth." (Genesis 1:1)

If God was before all things, then out of what did He create all things? God always creates out of Himself, and God creates everything for Himself. God is all in all. Thus His omnipotence does not violate His own creative principle.

God is being. Everything begins in God. Likewise, everything begins in your God-self, whether good, bad, or indifferent. Believe it or not, **all** things have their beginning in you. Isaiah 45:7 says, *"I formed the light and created darkness. I make peace and create evil. I, the Lord, do all these things."*

Your outward experiences are only a manifestation of what is taking place on the inside of you. As you begin to understand your being, you will move forward in His likeness.

God made man in His image and after His likeness. Therefore, God, the Creator of all things, came to reveal Himself so that you can operate in your "God-self." However, your "God-self" only operates when you go within yourself. The Bible says, *"I am God and beside me there is no other."* (Deuteronomy 4:35) In order to operate effectively in your "God-self" you must divorce the mindset of another god, or a God outside of you. Otherwise, you will never walk in victory. You will never experience prosperity. You will never experience divine health and peaceful living. When you understand that you are the creator of all things, then you can share this truth with others. As you begin to discover the truth about yourself and the truth of your being, you will realize that you are more than who you think.

You create the world in which you live, whether it is a world of lack or a world of prosperity, a world of sadness or a world of joy, a world of sickness or a world of divine health. The world will always mirror **YOU**! Whatever lack you experience on the outside reveals the lack that is within **YOU**!

∼

PRINCIPLE #1

*All things have their beginning in you,
whether good, bad or indifferent.*

∼

God said, *"Let there be light, and there was light."* (Genesis 1:3) Light could not be unless God let it be. In the same way, nothing can "be" in your life unless you let it be. You cannot lose your job, unless you let "unemployment" be. You cannot lose your spouse, unless you let "divorce" be. You cannot lose your home, unless you let "homelessness" be. You cannot be poor, unless you let "poverty" be. You cannot be sick, unless you let "sickness" be. You cannot prosper, unless you let "prosperity" be. You will only experience the level that you LET. If you don't **LET IT BE**, you will not experience it!

If you don't LET IT BE, you will not experience it!

"Let every soul be subject unto the higher powers. For there is no power but of God: the powers that be are ordained of God." (Romans 13:1)

There is only **ONE** power. There is no power outside of God. God forms the light, yet He creates darkness. Light is really a form. Darkness is created, but light is formed. Light allows you to see on this realm, but darkness represents the unseen realm, the place where creation happens. Again, the scripture says, *"I make peace and create evil.* (Notice, God created evil.) *I, the Lord, do all these things." (emphasis added)*

So, any "evil" that exists in our lives, it is God in us who created it. God creates peace and He creates evil. That is the beauty of life. Before we came into being, we were in heaven where there was all good. However, we came to earth to experience good and evil. Adam would not have been complete just eating from the tree of life. He wanted to experience eating from the tree of the knowledge of good and evil. And after he ate of it, God said, *"Man has become like one of us, knowing good and evil."* (Genesis 3:22)

There is only one power. The only devil you will ever meet is the "devil" in you that is ignorant of the God-power that is resident on the inside of you. Your outward experiences are only a manifestation of what is taking place on the inside of you. The universe is a mirror of who you are. The world will always mirror <u>YOU</u>! You create the world in which you live. Whether a world of lack or a world of prosperity, you create that world. The only reason you may not receive something is because you lack receiving it. The lack within you rejects its coming. Therefore, if you lack prosperity, it is because you have not given yourself permission to prosper.

The same God who created the laws of gravity also created the laws of prosperity. Poverty is a state of consciousness. Poverty has nothing to do with the amount of money you have in the bank, or the house, neighborhood, community, or surroundings in which you live. In the same way, prosperity is also a state of consciousness. Prosperity has nothing to do with the number of vehicles you own, or if you own a vehicle at all. This is not your reality. Your reality is not the things that you possess. Prosperity is consciousness. Your reality is consciousness.

$\sim$

PRINCIPLE #2

Whatever you lack on the outside
reveals the lack that is within you!

$\sim$

Ross Perot, a wealthy man, chose not to drive a brand new vehicle, although he could afford to drive any vehicle he desired. His prosperity gave him the power to *choose.* In the

4

same way, you have the power to choose your level of living. You choose your reality, and the reality that you choose becomes the reality that is within you. The work must take place in your consciousness. God is your reality. Prosperity is not only related to finances, but you must prosper physically, emotionally, and spiritually in order to achieve wholeness in your life. Remember, "In the beginning, God."

The moment you realize that God is your reality; you will demonstrate God as reality. Rest in your reality and realize that reality is not materiality. God, the Creator of all things, comes to reveal Himself, so that you can operate in your God-self, for God made man in His image and after His likeness.

Jesus said to the Apostle Peter, *"Who do you say that I am?"* Jesus was waiting for Peter to say something that resonated within Him. Peter responded, *"You are the Christ, the Son of the living God."* Jesus responded, *"Okay, Peter, you have it right, and upon that I will build my Church."* (Matthew 16:15-16)

The law of perception is powerful. What you perceive, your "I Am" within you is creating. The "I", who is God, cannot be seen unless there is an object (or a person). The "I" must be objectified for the demonstration of God's hand to be seen. The truth within you echoes that which you perceive. The "I Am" in you is creating the object outside of you. Unless your reality is aligned with God's reality, you will find yourself chasing after things instead of being anchored in the kingdom.

The God-self only operates when you go within. If you look for a God outside of you, you will be guilty of dwelling in idolatry. Scripture says *"I am God, and beside me there is no other."* You must get out of the mindset of another god or you will not walk in victory, nor will you experience prosperity, which only happens when you operate in your God-self.

Therefore, you must connect to a prophet, one who can speak into your life the destiny that God has designed just for you. However, you can only move into your prophetic destiny to the degree of your own faith. You don't want someone with little faith trying to prophesy big things in your life. You want someone who understands the principle that you are the creator of all things. Then, and only then, will you start creating that same faith in another. You have to give the principle away in order for the principle to live.

~

PRINCIPLE #3

ALL things have their beginning in you!

~

Believing vs. Knowing

The story is told of a man who once asked a preacher an important question. The man asked, *"Do you believe in God?"* The preacher replied, *"No. When you know God, you do not have to believe in God. This question suggests the notion that I am separate and apart from the "Self", who I am. I do not have to demonstrate my belief in God, because I know God."*

We are living in an Age where God is moving His people from believing to knowing.

The Bible says, *"Thou believest that there is one God; thou doest well: the devils also believe and tremble."* (James

6

2:19) <u>Belief</u> does not get you anything, because even the devils believe and tremble.

This is an Age where God is moving His people from "believing" to "knowing." We have moved out of a Piscean Age, which was an age of believing, into an Aquarian Age, which is an age of knowing or knowledge, and which some term as the "New Age." Every 2,000 to 2,500 years we come into a new age. The Internet is a tool that we use today to acquire knowledge and information concerning various subjects. Often referred to as the "Information Super-Highway", its purpose is solely information. We are in an age of information, an age of knowledge, an age of knowing. We are in a New Age.

> *This is an Age where God is moving His people from "believing" to "knowing."*
>
> ~

Jesus represented the New Age of His day. It was the end of the Aries Age, the end of the Age of the Ram. Why do you think Abraham saw a ram caught in the thicket? Why the ram? Because it was the Age of the Ram. It was the Ram that came to take away the sins of the world. *"Behold, the Lamb of God (the Ram) which hath come to take away the sins of the world* (everything that caused you to miss the mark).*"* (John 1:29, emphasis added)

Jesus was introducing a Piscean Age. He said to His disciples, *"I will make you fishers of men."* (Matthew 4:19) He also said, *"I will give unto you the sign of the Prophet Jonah,"* which was the sign of the big fish. (Luke 11:29) Why were the early Christians going around drawing the symbol of the fish? Because the Pharisees and Sadducees of their day considered them a New Age community. At that time, it was not fashionable to be a Christian. As a result, they were persecuted. They were mocked because they represented the New Age of their day.

Today represents the end of a Piscean Age and the beginning of an Aquarian Age. The Aquarian Age is an Age of Knowing, an Age of Knowledge. When we understand the Age in which we stand, we will begin to understand more prophetically the Aquarian Age and what it represents. In this Age we are not supposed to <u>believe in</u> God; we are supposed to <u>know</u> God. However, you can only know that which you are. You do not have to demonstrate your belief in God because you are God, not in personality, but in principle. How well do you know Him?

~

PRINCIPLE #4

When you <u>know</u> God, you do not have to <u>believe in</u> God.

~

Demonstrate Dominion

God wants us to think universally and have a global reach. God does not want you to think locally. Jesus was not a local boy. Jesus was universal in His approach. His message was universal. He had a global perspective. The world has become a village. When you begin to think and see from a universal perspective, you will start speaking your truth from a universal connection.

Psalm 82:1-3 says, *"God standeth in the congregation of the mighty; he judgeth among the gods. How long will we judge unjustly, and accept the persons of the wicked? Defend the poor and fatherless; do justice to the afflicted and needy."* The Amplified Bible says, "God stands in the assembly [of the representatives]..." God only stands in what represents ("re-presents") Him. You should be God's representative, because you "re-present" the Lord. You are the presence of the Lord "doing over again" ("re") that which God is. Repeat these words, *"The Lord is here."* How can you say the Lord is here? Because you "re-present" God.

Psalm 82:4-6 says, *"Deliver the poor and needy: rid them out of the hand of the wicked. They know not, neither will they understand; they walk on in darkness: all the foundations of the earth are out of course. I have said, Ye are gods; and all of you are children of the most High."* If you do not believe the fact that you are a god, then you do not know God. If you <u>believe in</u> God, then you don't <u>know</u> God. You may have Him separate and apart from yourself.

We are in an Age where God is pouring out His Spirit upon all flesh, and your sons and your daughters <u>will</u> prophesy. Some people believe that this will occur in the "last days", according to Acts 2:17. However, when the Bible refers to the "last days" it means the last days of that particular age, that particular time, that particular era. But we are in a New Age, an age where God is going to reveal the mystery of His Word to the prophets, so that His prophets can take His people to a new level in Him and a new level in their prophetic destiny.

People are responsible for getting you into the situations that you are in today. You cannot sin by yourself. There has to be someone to expose you to the decay of life. There has to be someone to party with, to sleep with, and to do drugs with. You don't sin by yourself. The drug addict did not become addicted to drugs by himself. He had to go to the drug dealer to obtain the drugs to which he is addicted. The drug dealer provided access to that which caused great pain in the drug addict's life. Similarly, you need a person to get you out of the situations that you are in. People get you into situations, and it will take people to get you out.

~

PRINCIPLE #5

God only stands in what represents Him.

~

Pain is a signal that you need someone. Just like the drug addict had to find the person who could supply him the drugs, you have to find the person who can give you the healing ingredient for your life. Sometimes your ego won't allow you to find the person who can help you because you are determined to do it on your own. But it is going to take a prophet (a person) to get you out of the confusion that you are in and into the Divine Purpose of God. That is the Power of Prophecy!

"...Let us make man in our image, after our likeness: and let them have dominion over the fish of the sea..." (Genesis 1:26) God created man for the purpose of having dominion. If you don't understand your purpose, you will be disillusioned and unable to exercise your true rulership, because whatever situations you don't have control over, those situations will have control over you.

One way in which people fail to understand their purpose of demonstrating dominion in the earth is by operating out of a principle of lack. God puts your treasure in an earthen vessel. However, many people look up into the sky for a "treasure" that is hidden in an "earthen vessel." Until you understand from where God brings the harvest, you will not work the "field." If you want to work the "field," then get into your earthen vessel.

Notice that treasures in the natural earth are in the deep. You have to go into the deep to find gold and diamonds. Pearls are in the deep. In order for an oyster to produce a pearl, the oyster must endure the intrusion of an irritant in its mouth. The irritant is under pressure, but in time it will become a pearl.

Moving Together As One

"...Let them have dominion over the fish of the sea, and over the fowl of the air, and over the cattle, and over all the earth, and over every creeping thing that creepeth upon the earth. So God created man in His own image, in the image of God created he him, male and female created he them." (Genesis 1:26-27)

One of man's greatest downfalls is that we do things in isolation. God did not make man in isolation. Some people are trying to work their miracle in isolation. When Elisha told the woman to go and borrow vessels, and not just a few, she knew that she could not fulfill the prophet's request alone. (1 Kings 4:1-6) She was sensible enough to (1) call on her sons and (2) send her sons to borrow pots from others. You cannot work miracles in isolation.

You cannot come into wealth through isolation, regardless of how tirelessly you work. Talk to any smart business person and he will tell you that he did not become wealthy independently. He assembled a team, and together they found customers and clients. They were in the business of pleasing someone else.

~

PRINCIPLE #6

You cannot work miracles in isolation.

~

Consider Jesus' miracles. Even Jesus did not multiply the fishes and loaves until He found a young lad whose lunch he could borrow. Where are your partners? Can you work on a team? What are your behavior patterns? What are you demonstrating to the world if you cannot stay connected to a team?

The prophets in Scripture were known as the Company of Prophets or the Sons of Prophets. The prophets traveled in bands. The wise men traveled as a group to see the Christ child. There were not three wise men, as portrayed in Christmas cards, but there were approximately 50 wise men traveling in a caravan. That is why they had gold, frankincense and myrrh. What do you have to bring to the Christ child? If your response is "nothing", then it is because you are traveling alone.

Birds are conscious of working together as a team. When they fly south, they fly together in a group. When the lead bird becomes tired, he drops to the back and the next bird takes the lead. However, you always see one bird flying off by himself. It would be better if the bird would stay in line with the other birds.

Why does a person move away from the team? Because he refuses to allow his ego to die. You must check your ego. Ego means simply "easing or edging God out." When ego takes over, God is moved out altogether, and you begin to operate in isolation. However, God has someone who is holding your treasure in an earthen vessel, and it is your responsibility to discern who it is and where they are in order to draw your treasure out of them. This is the reason God disturbed the prophet and told him to go to the widow woman at Zarephath. There is a treasure in you and a treasure in her. And until you go into the deep of each other, you will both be in lack. (1 Kings 17:9-16)

> *The only reason you are in lack is because you don't know how to connect with others.*
> ~

The only reason you are in lack is because you don't know how to connect with others. You want to operate as a soloist. If you cannot be on a team, think like a team, and function like a team, then you will miss your "treasure."

You may be pushing people aside who contain your treasure, yet they are not aware that they contain your treasure. They are in your midst wondering, "Why am I here?" Yet you stand in their midst clueless about their discontent, disliking the external package, and unable to discern the mind of God in them.

However, your treasure is in an earthen vessel, but you have to work the "field." You must make time to work the

13

"field." You must begin to say, *"I know a diamond when I see it. Give me a year, and I will produce a product."*

~

PRINCIPLE #7

*Your treasure is in an earthen vessel,
but you have to work the field.*

~

God always houses your blessing in someone who is close to you. He didn't send Noah all over the world to get the animals. The animals came to him. Someone is in route to you right now with your treasure in him, yet he does not know the reason for his coming to you. However, if you dwell in the "far country," you will miss the treasure that is sitting in the earthen vessel. There are no accidents in the universe. According to Beryl Wolk, "A coincidence is God's way of staying anonymous." Coincidences are God's anonymous visitations that occur in your life for the purpose of seeing if you can discern Him and praise Him. How many coincidences have you had in life?

~

PRINCIPLE #8

Whatever you perceive, your I Am, is creating.

~

CHAPTER 2

DIVINITY IS IN ME

—• ⫶✦⫶ •—

Original Righteousness

"But seek ye first the kingdom of God, and his right-eousness; and all these things shall be added. (Matthew 6:33)

Many people go to church and profess to be spiritual; however, many do not possess the kingdom. They do not operate in kingdom principles. The scripture clearly says to seek first the kingdom of God, and then the "things" will be added unto you. How many Bible-believing, church-going, Holy Ghost-filled people do you know living in lack, poor health, poverty and sadness? However, this is contrary to the system that God established in the beginning.

It is vital to develop a kingdom mindset if you want to reign as Christ in the earth. You have to begin to walk in victory and talk in victory. You have to live the kingdom and understand that the kingdom of God is within you. What are

15

you doing with the kingdom that is within you? How are you living? Are you living by kingdom principles or are you living as an earthling? What is important to you, the kingdom or your standard of living?

You must seek first the principles that govern the kingdom of God. Until you find the principles that govern the kingdom of God, you will not see the manifestation of God. God cannot manifest until you get in principle. You are God in principle. But it is important to understand that you are God in principle, not in personality.

> *"God is the creator of all things. From the outset of the Book of Genesis, the focus of the strong light of revelation turns upon the Almighty. He is the Beginning, the Cause, the Source of all that is. He brought into being all the things and the persons that were to fit into his plan for the ages. All the matter necessary for his later working, he miraculously created."* (The Wycliffe Bible Commentary, Electronic Database)

God made all things out of Himself. Even Himself is out of Himself. God created man in His own image. Therefore, there is no original sin. There is only original righteousness, because God created man originally Him. It is a natural instinct of man to be like God. It is not natural for man to walk in sin. You may say, *"Well, the Psalmist David said, 'I was born in sin and shaped in iniquity.'"* When David said, "I was born in sin," maybe he was talking about the relationship. He was not talking about universal man; David was talking about himself.

16

~

PRINCIPLE # 9

You are God in principle, NOT in personality.

~

You are originally righteous. God made man in His image, after His likeness, originally righteous, but then man chose to fall. Man chose to walk away from his righteousness and be the devil, because he was tired of being God. What is the difference between God and the devil? There is only one power.

The devil is God twisted a twisted concept of the Almighty. The devil is your own self-ignorance. Remember the prodigal son? (Luke 15:11-32) The prodigal son asked for his inheritance. The sin was not him asking for his inheritance. The sin was him divorcing himself from the root. The father told him, "All that I have is yours." So, if all that the father had belonged to the son, then it was not wrong for the son to have all that he had, he just did not want him to be separated from the root. The sin of the prodigal son was that he was separated from his father's economy. As long as you keep separating yourself from the Father's economy, you are lost.

Creating My State Of Affairs

What have you sought first in life? Has it been the King or has it been something else?

Psalm 119:130 says, *"The entrance of thy words giveth light. It giveth understanding unto the simple."* There are many people who have lost the power of understanding because they have become dull in hearing. When you lose your ability to hear and to understand, you don't know what to do with wisdom. What good is wisdom if you don't understand what wisdom is? What good is wisdom if you don't know how to apply it? What good is wisdom if you don't know how to work it? *"Get wisdom, and with all thy getting get understanding."* (Proverbs 4:7)

Things do not get added to you until you seek first the kingdom. Why does God add things to you? So that the Gentiles will come seeking the things and find the kingdom in you. The kingdom is not in outer space. There is no God "out there" that can help you. Stop looking out there! There is no God "up there" that can help you. Stop looking up there!

The Bible says, Jesus lifted up his eyes. He lifted up His eyes from the realm in which He was standing, to the realm in which He needed to see supply. It was not a physical lifting up of the eye, as much as it was a spiritual lifting of seeing from one realm into the next. Heaven is not up in a physical direction. If it were, then you should be able to take a rocket and get there. Neither is heaven in a geographical location. If it were, you would be able to get there by some means of transportation. Heaven is a realm, not a place in space.

~

PRINCIPLE #10

Do not separate yourself from the Father's economy.

~

The only mansion you will ever see is the mansion that is here on planet earth. There are no mansions in heaven.

18

What need is there for a mansion in heaven when heaven is a spiritual place? Even Jesus said to the two men, *"Why stand ye here gazing?"* (Acts 1:11) Some people have been left gazing. For this same Jesus is coming in like manner. The same Jesus is coming like you. Many people are gazing out, when they need to be gazing within, because Jesus is coming just like you!

Your state of mind is always creating your state of affairs.

If hell is below, then how far do we have to go into the earth to find hell? There is no power outside of the "self." Your state of mind is always creating your state of affairs. You have to get your mind back to the place where you are focused, and then you will create focused opportunities.

Adversity is the breeding ground for miracles. If adversity is present in your life, you are next in line for a miracle. Life changes only when you change your daily priorities. Your habits create your character, and your character will determine your destiny. Your daily activities reveal where you are going. Your "net-work" determines your "net worth." How much money do you have the potential of making? Look at who you are in relationship with and it will reveal your salary. The question is not, who do you work for, but who do you work with that is on an equal level? Just because you work in the bank doesn't mean you have access to the vault. The janitor has the key to the bank, but he doesn't have access to the vault. You can be sleeping with someone and not dream the same dream, though you sleep on the same pillow.

19

∽

PRINCIPLE #11

*Look at who you are in relationship with,
and it will reveal your salary.*

∽

If you want to create a new destiny for yourself, you must assist others in becoming successful. You must also assist others in discovering their gifts, because you reap what you sow. Job 42:10 says, *"...And the Lord turned the captivity of Job when he prayed for his friends; also the Lord gave Job twice as much..."* Your captivity will not turn until you do something. Job went through a process. Job had to pray for his friends. His friends thought he had done something wrong. Have you ever considered maybe it was a process? Have you ever considered maybe this was a test? God never gives you wisdom unless He is going to present a problem.

The Lord gave Job twice as much as He had before. Do you want twice as much? I dare you to pray for those that have mistreated you. There are going to be some people for whom you will have to pray and with whom you cannot be bitter afterwards. Everyday you go through a death. But you have to say, *"Okay, here you come. Come on, stab me in the back. Go on, fulfill your sacred mission. Crucify me afresh so I can resurrect in power!"*

Some people have been assigned to your life to keep you down, only to witness your resurrection. However, you must value the people in your life. Even God uses Satan for His purpose. There may be someone in your life that is operating like Satan, trying to thwart the plan of God in your life; use them for God's purpose. Every devil is not to be destroyed. There are some devils you are supposed to keep around because they are going to bring the next harvest to you.

If the wealth of the wicked is laid up for the righteous, then we need a certain amount of wicked, do we not? God is all in all. There is only one power. Therefore you must speak your expectation of success, not your experiences of failure. Failure becomes disappointment and then despair. But God wants to turn your disappointments into appointments.

~

PRINCIPLE #12

Adversity is the breeding ground for miracles.

~

Your Power To Create

"This parable spake Jesus unto them, but they under-stood not what things they were which he spake unto them. Then Jesus said unto them again, 'Verily, verily I say unto you, I am the door of the sheep. All that ever came before me are thieves and robbers, but the sheep did not hear them. "I am the door: by me if any man enter in, he shall be saved, and shall go in and out, and find pasture." (John 10:6-9)

Anything that enters your life without your permission is a thief. Therefore, you must declare all things in the con-sciousness of "I Am" so that nothing or no one can rob you of the true essence of your being. When you understand that you are the door, then everything that comes through you is saved and safe because you keep it based on the level of your consciousness, or the level of your experience.

John 10:10 says, *"The thief cometh not, but for to steal, and to kill, and to destroy: I am come that they might have life and that they might have it more abundantly."* Jesus came that you might have life, and have it more abundantly. If you don't understand the coming of the Lord for the purpose of you having life, you will miss God in your life altogether. Notice who was coming - "I Am." It was not really Jesus in personality.

Remember the rich young ruler said unto Jesus, *"Good Master, what shall I do to inherit eternal life?"* and Jesus said, *"Why callest thou me good?"* (Luke 18:18-19) Jesus was trying to redirect the young ruler away from His personality. Jesus was not saying that He is the door. He was letting you know the door is "I Am". The door is the principle of the consciousness of "I Am", and "I Am" happened to manifest Himself and call Himself Jesus; and we know that Jesus is the savior of all men. Jesus really came to reveal your "self," not so much Himself. This teaching alone should lift you to a new realm of consciousness in Christ.

～

PRINCIPLE #13

Anything that enters your life without permission is a thief.

～

"I am the good shepherd: the good shepherd giveth his life for the sheep. But he that is a hireling, and not the shepherd, whose own the sheep are not, seeth the

wolf coming, and leaveth the sheep, and fleeth, and the wolf catcheth them, and scattereth the sheep. The hireling fleeth because he is a hireling and careth not for the sheep."

(John 10:11-13)

When you are a hireling, you work for pay, not for the love. You run when the wolf shows up. That is why it's important for you to understand the spirit of consciousness. Are you doing work that you love or are you doing work for hire? It's the same principle. You will never become wealthy doing work that you are hired to do. You will only be wealthy doing work that you love, because when you find your love, you will find God, for God is love. If you want God in your work, then you must do the work that you love.

Until you find work that you love, you will be in poverty. Wealth only comes from "love work", because it is no longer work, it is your love. For example, I prophesy to you not because I'm hired to prophesy. I prophesy because I love to prophesy. I love to prophesy because that is what God birthed in me. If you are working to pay bills, then there is no love in it. If you seek the love, then the bills will be paid. If you work just to work, then you will be miserable. If you work because you love your work, then you have found your sacred mission. Find your love and do it.

～

PRINCIPLE #14

*Until you find work that you love,
you will be in poverty.*

～

John 10:14-16 says, *"I am the good shepherd, and know my sheep, and am known of mine. As the Father knoweth me, even so know I the Father, and I lay down my life for the sheep. And other sheep I have, which are not of this fold, them also I must bring, and they shall hear my voice; and there shall be one fold and one shepherd."* In other words, no one is going to really be lost. Even the sheep that were not of His fold, God said, "Them also I must bring." God declared that there shall be one fold, because there is only one God. There is no power outside of the power of God.

There is no power outside of the power of God.

~

God is sovereign. He created man in His own image, after His likeness. Before God sent you to the earth realm, He made you sign a contract. He made a covenant with you of the things you were supposed to fulfill while here on planet earth. He gave you instructions for fulfilling His plan. God didn't bless Adam and Eve after they got here. He had already blessed them in His imagination. In the same way, you have already been blessed with all spiritual blessings in heavenly places. Therefore, you do not have to wait to receive a blessing. The only reason you are trying to receive a blessing is because you fell from the grace of remembering that you are a blessing.

"...and God said unto them, Be fruitful, and multiply, and replenish the earth, and subdue it: and have dominion over the fish of the sea, and over the fowl of the air, and over every living thing that moveth upon the earth. And God said, Behold, I have given you

every herb bearing seed, which is upon the face of the earth, in every tree, in the which is the fruit of a tree yielding seed; to you it shall be for meat. And to every beast of the earth, and to every fowl of the air, and to every thing that creepeth upon the earth, wherein there is life, I have given every green herb for meat, and it was so. And God saw every thing that he made, and, behold, it was very good."

(Genesis 1:28-31)

When God created man, He created him from the highest vibration He could function with at that season. It was His very image. On the first day, God created light, which was the lower form of vibration, and then the vibration kept increasing each day until He created man and He said, "It is very good." The day God created man was the only day He said that it was "very good." So, guess what you are? Very good. You may say, "But wait, the Bible says call no man good. There is only one good and that is God." Guess who you are? God! You are very good. You are "very God."

In the same way, you create in the imagination of God, and then you have to give your creation instructions. God gave man his instructions (his purpose) while he was Spirit. When God judges you, He judges you for not remembering what your assignment was in your pre-incarnated state. You are judged for being at the wrong longitude and latitude and operating outside of His purpose and plan for your life.

That is why you need the prophet in your life, to discern the plan of God for your life and to remind you of your instructions. When the prophet speaks the word of the Lord, he has your contract in his mind. For example, I looked at Rev. Run's contract in the Spirit and said, "Okay, Rev. Run, I know you were a rapper, but you are supposed to be doing sneakers. You are supposed to be working in Phat Farm. You are supposed to be in clothing." At the time, Rev. Run did not understand this word. However, he did not throw it away, he did not cancel it in the spirit, nor did he reject its coming. Instead, he took the Word and put it in his "I don't understand file." Then God caused a season of events to take place and Rev. Run said, "Oh, the prophet was reading the contract right, I just forgot." Today, he is the owner of a very successful sneaker company, a division of Phat Farm.

Therefore, never cancel out your contract with God. Although you may not understand the prophetic word, know that God will reveal it to you in time.

~

PRINCIPLE #15

Never cancel out your contract with God.

~

CHAPTER 3

IT'S DARK IN HERE!

I Don't Understand!

"In the beginning God created the heaven and the earth. And the earth was without form, and void; and darkness was upon the face of the deep.

And the Spirit of God moved upon the face of the waters." (Genesis 1:1-2)

God begins everything in darkness. He initiates everything from within Himself. The richness is in the darkness. The richness is in your ability to unmask your ignorance and find your way into the light. When God begins to prepare you for a new day, a new visitation, a new way of expressing Himself through you, in you, and as you, He will always bring you into the "darkroom." However, when you step into the newness of God, it may appear as if you have no clue of what you are doing.

Why would the Spirit of God move upon the face of the deep unless something can come out of the deep? The "deep" represents your subconscious, or the part of you that is invisible. The Spirit of God is always moving upon your deep, searching out the inward secrets, or the inward laws of your heart. The Spirit is searching out your "deep" and bringing it forth so that it can be revealed in your time, and in your place.

God will always push you into something that will showcase your ignorance just so that you can say, "It must be God. I don't understand what is going on." For example, when God told Abraham, "I want to send you into a land that I will show you," Abraham did not know where he was going. Likewise, Joseph had a dream. He saw his brothers, his mother and his father bowing down to him, and he saw that he was going to be raised up as a leader among his people. He did not know where he was going, nor did he know the hell that he would go through.

Whenever God directs you, He always pushes you into darkness. God never reveals what He will take you <u>through</u>, but He will reveal what He will bring you <u>to</u>. He may not give you the details, because the person to whom He gives the word is not the same person in whom He fulfills the word. You may be a different person altogether when the Word finally comes to pass.

~

PRINCIPLE #16

God begins everything in darkness.

~

You may receive a prophetic word; however, you are a different person when you walk out that word. You are not the same person that you were when you received the word. You may have the same body, but you have a completely different makeup. You are evolving into a whole new state of being. You are coming into a new awareness. Therefore, the person to whom He gives the word is not the same person in whom He fulfills the word.

He spoke His word to an Abram, but He fulfilled it in Abraham. He spoke His word to a Sarai, but He fulfilled it in Sarah. He spoke His word to Jacob, but fulfilled it in Israel. He spoke His word to Joseph, when Joseph was in his father's house, in a coat of many colors, but He fulfilled it in Joseph's life when he was Prime Minister of Egypt. He spoke His word to Moses as a babe, and fulfilled it in Moses, who, upon being kicked out of Pharaoh's court onto the back side of the desert, returned 80 years later demanding "let my people go." When a person receives a prophetic word, they receive the word as they are, but God fulfills that word in another incarnation.

God always speaks to the person inside of you, the one whom you have yet to discover. God only speaks to your potential. However, many people get frustrated because they try to walk in their potential at the moment it is revealed without going through the gestation period, or the mentoring process. They refuse to sit under the guidance of a mentor in order to learn how to effectively move and operate in their potential. Many people will jump out of the womb of preparation before their full development. As a result, they abort their assignment (destiny). However, you must stay in the womb of preparation until the full incarnation, after that gestation, and then you will be in a new present situation.

You will have to go through a process in order to come into the materialization of the prophetic word and what God is saying concerning you. Are you really ready for what God is saying? Many people say, "Let's go to the other side," however, they are comfortable on this side. Many people say, "Lord, take me into that place. Take me to the next level," however, they find themselves carrying a lot of baggage because they did not understand the prophetic word. God is saying, "Do you understand?"

~

PRINCIPLE #17

God only speaks to your potential.

~

The Great Divide

> *"And God said, let there be light: and there was light. And God saw the light, that it was good: and God divided the light from the darkness." (Genesis 1:3-4)*

Light is hidden in darkness. Isn't it interesting that God divided the light from the darkness? It appears that darkness was there before light was created. In the above passage of scripture, the word "light" is not referring to the sun, moon, and stars. The sun was not created until the fourth day. Although there is a form of light known as sunlight, God's reference to "light" in this passage of scripture is another form of light.

Many people have tapped into only one aspect of light, and have never met God as light. God is light, and He hides His treasure, or His good, in dark places. God divided the light from the darkness. The "One" is always turning Himself into the "many." He said, "Let there be light," and then He divided. Why would he say, "Let there be light," and then divide it. Why would He let there be one, and then divide it into two?

Whenever God gives you something, He gives it to you for the purpose of dividing it, to demonstrate His wholeness and His boldness in you. God divided the light from the darkness. The darkness He called Night, and the light He called Day. And then we see the evening and the morning made the first day.

> *Until there is the "pulling apart", there cannot be the creating of more.*
>
> ~

God multiplies through you by dividing. For example, He may give you $100 and then tell you to give away $50, because He is getting ready to bless you with more than $100. That is the science of God. Look how many days were created after God divided the light from the darkness. A day did not exist until He divided the day from the night. There was only one day and it was eternity, but there wasn't succession of days until the evening and the morning came and made the first day. Until there is the "pulling apart", there cannot be the creating of more.

Sometimes we try to keep what God has given us as one entity, but we need to divide it and break it so there can be more. That is how you multiply. Jesus took the bread and lifted it. He raised the vibration of the bread and then he broke it. Why did Jesus break the bread? There were 5,000 hungry men, not counting women and children, and if he did not break the bread and decided to keep it whole, He would have never been able to feed the masses.

"And God said, "Let there be a firmament in the midst of the waters, and let it divide the waters from the waters." (Genesis 1:6)

God created a firmament in the midst of the waters, and then He turns around and divides it. Grab onto God's principle of multiplying by dividing.

For example, you should not shoulder the weight of your purpose alone, for it is too great for you to do by yourself. If you mother it, you will smother it. If you allow everything to rest on your shoulders, then you will die prematurely. Many of our leaders die early because there is no distribution of management. People want to be plugged into just one person. However, they do not understand that God puts His glory in a corporate body. God gives the vision to one man, but then there are other men and women who are supposed to catch the vision and shoulder it.

~

PRINCIPLE #18

God multiplies through you by dividing.

~

"And God made the firmament, and divided the waters which were under the firmament from the waters which were above the firmament: and it was

so. And God called the firmament Heaven. And the evening and the morning were the second day." (Genesis 1:7-8)

On the second day there was a great amount of division occurring. There is division that brings life, but then there is also division that brings death. This division that occurred on the second day occurred in heaven, where God is One. The earth is for the "One" to become the "many," but when we leave the earth it is for the "many" to go back into the "One."

Emerging From The Dark

"...And God divided the light from the darkness. And God called the light Day, and the darkness He called Night. And the evening and the morning were the first day." (Genesis 1:4-5)

God divided light from darkness. Light came out of darkness. The evening and the morning made the first day, which means that a new day starts in the evening and ends in the morning. Whenever God starts a new day in your life it will begin in darkness. It will begin in uncertainty. It will begin in a place where you have no understanding of what God is doing. It will look like you are confused. It will look like God does not know what He is saying. It may even appear as if you missed it. But God always starts a new day in your life where you have to go through a season of ridicule and where you will be misunderstood.

God always starts a new day in your life where people are standing on the sidelines awaiting your failure. Your situation will seem chaotic. It will seem wrong. It will seem like everything is going left instead of right. But in the process of what God is doing, it will begin to take form and shape, and then you will begin to see it. You may say, "Lord, I need this." You may say, "Lord, I asked you for more wisdom and it seems like I'm getting more problems. Things are not working out the way that I thought." It seems as though you are not getting what you need. But how are you going to have wisdom to solve problems in other people's lives if you never experienced problems in your own life?

God's ways are not like man's ways. A lot of times we try to put God in a box and say, "Lord, I want you to do it this way." But when God is creating a new day it is not going to be the way you perceive it to be, nor will it be the way that you think it should be. God is creating and molding situations in your life so that you can be satisfied. But you must say, "Lord, not my will, but let thy will be done in and through me." Remember, God is the Creator.

~

PRINCIPLE #19

In the midst of your new day,
people are waiting to see you fail.

~

You have to learn to say, "Lord, I am just the vessel. I am just the instrument. Do whatever you see fit. Do as you please because you know the end result." Many people have a tendency to look at their present condition. But God is all in all. He knows the beginning from the end and the end from beginning. So when God is creating that new day that we may perceive to be dark, we may perceive it to be a day of disaster, a day of chaos, but in the midst of that, God is stirring because He is working in the dark.

If you take a glass of water and put juice or powder in it, it may look clear at first, but after you add the ingredients to it, the color changes. That is the same thing that God does. God will be stirring that day up for you because He knows just what you need. We are telling God, "Lord, I want this. I want that." But God is saying, "No, I know what is best for you." Daddy always knows what is best. Man might think, but God always knows.

Learn to rest in that which God is doing in your life.

There is a difference between thinking and knowing. You should not want what man thinks you should have, but you should want what God desires for you because He is the Creator, the Author, and the Finisher of your faith. Once you begin to say, "Lord, have thy way," that new day is going to come to you. When a new day comes, you should cease from your struggles. Learn to rest in that which God is doing in your life. Oftentimes people try to assist God in completing His work in them. However, we can't help God out or try to fix it because if we do, we will produce an "Ishmael", an offspring outside of the plan of God. (Genesis 16:11)

God knows the beginning and the end. When you begin to rest in God and begin to allow God to be who He is and what He is, the circumstances in your life will begin to go much smoother. You must say, "Lord, I don't understand it. I don't even see what you are doing. But, Lord, nevertheless, let thine will be done. Have thy own way in me, through me, and around me."

Your beginning may be in darkness, but God will bring you through the darkness and into the light. Once you understand the move of God, it behooves you to connect with those who understand God's movement. Step into the dark with them and rejoice in the darkness together, so that when you come into the light, you will not be the only one rejoicing. Instead you will find yourself looking for the next period of darkness, because you now understand how God moves.

~

PRINCIPLE #20

You should not want what man thinks you should have, but you should want what God desires for you.

~

There are many people who need light to understand the move of God. The Bible says, *"A wicked generation seeketh for a sign."* (Matthew 16:4) People look for something that they can handle, something that they can point to and say, "See." But you cannot point and tell people to see in the dark. What can they see? They can't see anything. But the evening and the morning make the first day. How can you tell someone to see something in the dark unless they are spiritual beings? They are unable to fully comprehend that the new day starts in the evening, in darkness. What they see looks like confusion.

If you are currently experiencing a problem in your life, know that your only problem is that you are blind to the answer. The answer is a gift that sits in your midst. However, you cannot see it because you do not know how to divide the light from the darkness in order to create a new day.

"The wealth of the wicked is laid up for the just." (Proverbs 13:22)

Light was "laid up" in darkness, like wealth is "laid up" in the wicked. God lays up wealth and treasures in the dark places. Unless you go through personal periods of testing, you will not have a testimony. You have to pass through a season of testing. You must pass through a season of "making." Darkness is the place of unformed purpose. Darkness is the place of development. When you go through a season of darkness, know that God is developing you. Just see the darkness and emerge from it!

Form It!

"And the Lord God formed man of the dust of the ground, and breathed into his nostrils the breath of life; and man became a living soul. And the Lord God planted a garden eastward in Eden; and there he put the man whom he had formed. And out of the ground made the Lord God to grow every tree that is pleasant to the sight, and good for food; the tree of life also in the midst of the garden; and the tree of knowledge of good and evil." (Genesis 2:7-9)

Everything is held in darkness waiting to be formed. However, many people do not function with what God has given them in the dark. The Bible says, *"Be not weary in well doing, for you will reap in due season if you faint not."*

(Galatians 6:9) Many people faint in the darkness and their dreams stay in the dark until they decide not to be afraid of the dark. You have to be willing to stand in the dark. Until you can stand in the dark, you are not spiritually mature. Everything that you need is in the dark. All you have to do is make it happen and bring it into the light.

God created the heavens and the earth, and the earth was without form. Whenever something is created it is always created 1) without form; 2) void; and 3) in the dark. It is not negotiable on the material plane. In the same way, the prophetic word is not formed; it is void; and it is not negotiable because it's all in the dark. Oftentimes, the prophet can be labeled as a false prophet because the prophet is seeing from one realm, while the natural man is looking from another realm.

~

PRINCIPLE #21

Your dreams are held in darkness
waiting to be formed.

~

If you don't understand the language of the prophetic or have a prophetic understanding, you will say something is not God because you don't see it with your natural eye. But no man has seen God at any time. Exodus 3:4 says, *"When the Lord saw that he had turned aside to see, God called unto him out of the midst of the bush, and said, Moses, Moses. And he said, here am I."* Moses very much wanted to see God. Exodus 3:6 says, *"Moreover he said, I am the God of thy father, the God of Abraham, the God of Isaac, and the*

God of Jacob. And Moses hid his face; for he was afraid to look upon God." If you look upon God as a natural man, you will be consumed, because only God can see God.

> *And he said, Thou canst not see my face: for there shall no man see me, and live."* (Exodus 33:20)

When you see God, you must become Him. You will no longer be able to live as man seeing God, because you become what you see.

> *"And the Lord said, Behold, there is a place by me, and thou shalt stand upon a rock: And it shall come to pass, while my glory passeth by, that I will put thee in a cleft of the rock, and will cover thee with my hand while I pass by. And I will take away mine hand, and thou shalt see my back parts: but my face shall not be seen."* (Exodus 33:21-23)

God said, *"You will see my back parts,"* you will see my effects. Most people today are seeing the effects of God and calling it God. People are really tripped up with the effects. The prophet must understand his role, which is to get in God's face. The prophet is the only office that speaks as God. The teachers teach you about the things of the Lord. The pastors lead the people back to the Lord, or pastor them and shepherd them. The prophets however declare a "thus saith the Lord!" The prophet's voice is always in the dark.

In Genesis 1, we see that the very thing that God created was without form. So, everything you create is without form. Everything you create is void. Everything you create is in darkness. Darkness is upon the very face of the deep thing that you just spoke.

Notice something, *"And the Spirit of God moved upon the very face of the waters."* When I look at the word "water" metaphysically, I see the emotions. Water symbolizes emotions. When we look at the creation story we understand that there are five kingdoms: the mineral kingdom, the vegetable kingdom, the animal kingdom, man's kingdom, and the kingdom of God. The earth represents the mineral kingdom. When we see the land appearing, that is the mineral. Then we see vegetation coming forth when he talks about the fruit trees yielding fruit after their kind. We see the animal kingdom when it talks about the fowl of the air. Then you have the kingdom of man. But ultimately, it's all the kingdom of God, which brings us into the seventh day, or the Sabbath. Which means the kingdom of God is eternally at rest.

~

PRINCIPLE #22

The kingdom of God is eternally at rest.

~

In Genesis 1, God is resting because the earth is without form and void. In reality, God is never really involved in things. Things are only your imagination. You represent the effects of God or the afterthoughts of God. We come to earth as the delay to bring about the effects in slow motion, so people can see the effects of God. We are always in the dark as man searching out for the form saying, "Why is my dream still void? Why is darkness still upon my deep thing?" until you come to the place where the Spirit of God in you begins to move upon the face of your emotions, or upon the face of your waters. Then you begin to become full of the feeling and start to operate in the law of assumption, where you begin to assume the very thing for which you pray. No prayer is ever answered until you assume the identity of it. Answered prayer is assumed identity. All prayers that are not answered are of mistaken identity.

Fulfillment comes first by the Spirit of God in you moving upon the face of your waters, upon the face of your emotions until you begin to emote, or move, or motion into the very form of the thing that you desire, and begin to start changing, or morphing into the very thing that you want to see fulfilled. I pray only to me, and then I change me by morphing into the very thing that I desire to be.

So, when you are hearing God, you are hearing yourself enlightened. *"I and my Father are one."* Psalm 110:1 says, *"The Lord said unto my Lord..."* God only talks to Himself. Any self-revelation you receive is you coming to a self-understanding or a self-revelation that "I am God." Now, your prayer is already answered. Who does God go to when He needs anything done? Himself. Who do you suppose to go to whenever you need something done? Yourself. So, why are you looking outside of yourself? That is idol worship. I don't care if your God is in the sky that is idol worship. You're into idolatry when you are looking outside of yourself for an answer that is right there within yourself.

~

PRINCIPLE #23

God only talks to Himself.

~

John 7:38 says, *"He that believeth on me, as the scriptures hath said, out of his belly shall flow rivers of living water"* First you have to believe on Him, as the scriptures have said. We are heirs of God and joint heirs of Jesus Christ. When you believe on Him you believe on yourself. Every scripture is about Jesus; therefore, every scripture is about you. Jesus didn't come here revealing Himself, but He came revealing yourself.

> *...manifestation is the movement of thought into mind.*
>
> ∼

Jesus said, *But this spake he of the Spirit, which they that believe on him should receive..."* (John 7:39) So, when you receive Him, or *"believe on Him, as the scripture hath said,"* then the Holy Ghost will flow out of you. Don't separate the Holy Ghost from the Holy Father and the Holy Son, because they are one. In our finite mind we seek to separate, which is where sin comes into play. Sin means separation. But in our eternal mind it's all one.

So, when God created, in Genesis 1, He is not disturbed that there is no form. He is not disturbed that there are no effects. So, why are we disturbed? Many of us get tripped up by effects. However, manifestation is the movement of thought into mind. The moment I thought about my first million, it was the movement of thought into mind. That was manifestation. The very first moment I desired a Rolls Royce that was a manifestation. Manifestation is just your ability to think it, to become pensive of it, to be able to reminisce, just to have the mind to do it.

The Bible says in Matthew 12:37, *"By the word thou shalt be justified, and by the word thou shalt be condemned."* Every word you speak out of your mouth about

42

yourself, you are either justifying yourself or you just condemned yourself. Condemnation and justification start in a
word, not in an act. "I am that house." "I am that thought."
"I am healed."

Revelation 4:11 says, *"Thou art worthy, O Lord, to
receive glory and honour and power: for thou hast created
all things..."* You are the creator of all things. All things that
are in your experience, you are the creator of them, because
God as Spirit really has no need of things. *"God is a Spirit
and they that worship him must worship him in Spirit and
in truth."*

In the beginning God could create heaven and earth; and
the earth was without form and void, and darkness was
upon the face of the deep, and God was still happy. You
make your happiness after the effects, when your happiness
is supposed to be happening in the movement of thought in
mind. The only things you create are the things that bring
you pleasure. Until you have pleasure in it in thought it
doesn't get created. Things are created by the pleasure of
your own will. A person suffers sickness because they plea-
sured it. It was their pleasure to imagine that tragedy. That
is why you have to ask yourself, what thoughts do you have
pleasure in?

~

PRINCIPLE #24

You must create your dream in your imagination.

~

You must create your dream in your own imagination, in
the darkroom, where it is without form and void. God loves

to have you in the place of uncertainty because you are operating in the dark. You're operating without material facts. You are operating in a realm where it is without form, where it is void, and darkness is upon the face of the deep. You are operating without a negotiable check. You are operating without negotiable means to make the outcome what it needs to be. Every true manifestation, everything that you get in your life, is done behind the scenes. That is why people say, "I don't understand how that happened to you." Visualization requires seeing in the dark. You must always get to a place where you can see in the dark.

So, a prophet of God is a prophet of secret. Amos 3:7 says, *"Surely the Lord God will do nothing, but he revealeth his secret unto his servants, the prophets."* The Lord God will do nothing, because everything God does is a secret. However, He will reveal his secrets to the prophet, so that the prophet can start moving the secret into the open. Whenever God needs the secret out, he gets it to a prophet, because the prophet is the only one that can utter the secrets of God.

~

PRINCIPLE #25

Until you find the principles that govern the kingdom of God, you will not see the manifestation of God.

~

Out Of Shape

God creates in the realm of the shapeless, the chaotic mass where usually Spirit is brooding over dark vapors.

44

Whatever you desire is chaotic and shapeless in the beginning. It is not yet formed. You may be unable to see it clearly because of the dark vapors. It is just a mist. It's just a thought, waiting for you to let it out of the darkness. It is waiting for you to free it. It is stuck in another realm and it has to be redeemed (freed) from that realm. However, you must set the captives free.

Your thoughts (your dreams) are trapped in prison (in the darkness) waiting for you to come with the key, unlock them, and say "Let there be!" Give them permission to come out, because they can only come out on your word. The Bible says, *"All of creation is waiting and groaning for the sons of God to manifest."* Could it be that God was demonstrating in creation what we are supposed to be doing right now, which is setting creation free?

God put Adam to sleep and brought forth Eve because Adam was tired of being alone. Adam's help came from within himself. In the same way, when you enter into sleep you enter into a state of meditation. You go back into the dark, into the place where Spirit hovers. That dark place can be seen as the place of your emotions, which can explain why there is moaning and groaning. Your dream is turning over and is looking for a way to form itself outside of you.

What is sitting on the inside of you that is waiting to be materialized? What is on the inside of you moaning and groaning, creating pain, doing somersaults within you, saying "Let us out of here! Get us out of the dark!" But for some reason you will not say, "Let there be light!" Creation is in limbo waiting for you to free your dream, free that thought, waiting for an expression, waiting for you to give birth to it. That is why it is groaning. That is why it is moaning. It is waiting for you to come forth and bring it out of its prison so that it can be free to grow, to express, and to be what God has ordained for it to be.

~

PRINCIPLE #26

Creation is in limbo waiting for you to give birth to your dream!

~

Life only serves you according to the form that has been cut out for this material realm, and then Spirit jumps into it. Everything must be pared out. Therefore, you should be so full of your dream the form becomes too big to stay on the inside of you.

P.U.S.H.!

When the prophet speaks into your life he creates forms and shapes. The prophet hears the Spirit, and then he has to take what he hears in Spirit and put shape and form to it so that the mind can catch it. However, God does not give birth to babies (vision). You have to birth your own vision. Don't get discouraged with your vision. Sometimes you give birth to the vision, but you don't feed it, clothe it, or nurture it, and as a result, your vision dies. It doesn't die in you, it dies outside of you. What are you doing with your vision after you birth it? Even when God gave birth to man, He put him in a garden and He gave him something to eat. He fed His vision. He created the right atmosphere and the proper environment for His vision to live.

When a woman is carrying a child, that child has everything it needs while it is in the mother's womb. The mother feeds it and nurtures it, and the child grows. But once the mother gives birth to the child and the mother and child go home, the house becomes an extension of the womb. The home is very important to the child's survival and well-being because the child still needs the very same nourishment. However, the child also needs hands-on care. When the child was in the womb, the mother could sleep and the child would still be nourished because the umbilical cord was attached to the child. Everything was happening involuntarily. But when the mother gives birth to the child, she must actively care for the child.

There comes a point in your life when you must realize that nobody is putting you through anything. You put yourself through whatever it is you are going through. Therefore, you have to P.U.S.H., prophesy until something happens. P.U.S.H. - Give birth to your dreams. P.U.S.H. - Give birth to your desires! P.U.S.H. - Give birth to your goals! P.U.S.H. - Give birth to the plans and purposes of God, because creation is waiting in eager expectation for the plan of God in your life to manifest!

~

PRINCIPLE #27

Prophesy until something happens.

~

CHAPTER 4

PROPHETS IN TRAINING

— ⊠⬧⊠ —

"But if I tarry long, that thou mayest know how thou oughtest behave thyself in the house of God, which is the church of the living God, the pillar and ground of the truth." (1 Timothy 3:15)

Divine Order

The Master Prophet (mentor) is the chief prophet of the house. He is the overseer, the one who is responsible for the spiritual well-being and overall operation of the house. The Sons (and Daughters) of the Prophet are those who are under the leadership, guidance and training of the Master Prophet, endeavoring to follow the principles, guidelines, and protocols as mandated by the Master Prophet.

There are timeless truths of divine order, structure and protocol-underlying ministry that are vital to the walk and the role of the prophet. There are also universal principles of service that govern the way in which the Son of the Prophet (mentee) must operate. Through recognition and submission to authority, the Son of the Prophet will render service unto the Master Prophet (mentor) that will yield him/her the grace to perform the Master Prophet's decrees.

If you are called to the prophetic ministry, I strongly encourage you to get training in the prophetic because it will help in building your character. As the mentee, your relationship with your mentor must be fueled by the desire to see the vision of your mentor live. These truths ultimately determine the strength of the ministry of the Son of the Prophet and his/her ability to demonstrate prophetically.

> *"And Saul sent messengers to take David: and when they saw the company of the prophets prophesying, and Samuel standing [as] appointed over them, the Spirit of God was upon the messengers of Saul, and they also prophesied."* (1 Samuel. 19:20)

Samuel was "appointed" over the company of prophets. During biblical times, the prophets traveled as a company. The New King James Version says that Samuel was "standing as the leader" over the company of prophets. The New American Standard Version says that Samuel was "standing and presiding" over the company of prophets.

Samuel was considered the Master Prophet. He was appointed to preside and stand as leader over the company of prophets. The company of prophets was seen as the troops. According to the New Living Translation, *"He sent troops to capture him. But when they arrived and saw Samuel and the other prophets prophesying, the Spirit of God came upon Saul's men and they began to prophesy."*

The prophets did not move in isolation. Isolation is a disease. The prophet needs order. Therefore, to foster order, he/she should operate within a company of prophets. If the prophet does not function within a company, then he/she is out of order. The Darby Bible translation reads, *"Then Saul sent messengers to take David, and they saw a company of prophets prophesying and Samuel standing as president over them..."* Every prophet should be able to point to a president or a senior officer under whom he/she operates. There cannot be a prophet if there is no head. Therefore, there must be some aspect of lineage to which a prophet is connected.

Whom Do I Serve?

"And the child Samuel ministered unto the Lord before Eli. And the word of the Lord was precious in those days; there was no open vision. And it came to pass at that time, when Eli was laid down in his place, and his eyes began to wax dim, that he could not see. And ere the lamp of God went out in the temple of the Lord, where the ark of God was, and Samuel was laid down to sleep; That the Lord called Samuel: and he answered, Here I am. And he ran unto Eli, and said, Here I am: for thou callest me. And he said I called not; lie down again. And he went and lay down. And the Lord called yet again, Samuel. And Samuel arose and went to Eli, and said; Here I am; for thou didst call me. And he answered, I called not, my son, lie down again. Now Samuel did not yet know the Lord..." (1 Samuel 3:1-7)

You can minister unto the Lord yet not know the word of the Lord. You can minister unto the Lord, but not hear the voice of the Lord. In other words, you can know the position of God, yet not know the principles of God. The position or office may be seen, yet the principles may not be recognized.

When Samuel ministered unto the Lord, he ministered unto authority. Romans 13:1-4, says, *"Let every soul be subject unto the higher powers. For there is no power but of God: the powers that be are ordained of God. Whosoever therefore resisteth the power resisteth the ordinances of God: and they that resist shall receive to themselves damnation. For rulers are not terrors to good works, but to the evil. Wilt thou then not be afraid of the power? Do that which is good, and thou shalt have praise of the same. For he is the minister of God to thee for good..."*

Who is the minister of God to thee for good? The individual who is in authority. God and delegated authority are inseparable, for there is no power but of God. All power is of God.

~

PRINCIPLE #28

God and delegated authority are inseparable.

~

"And It came to pass at that time, when Eli was laid down in his place, and his eyes began to wax dim, that he could not see; and ere the lamp of God went out in the temple of the Lord, where the ark of God was, and Samuel was laid down to sleep; That the Lord called Samuel, and he answered, Here am I. And he ran unto Eli, and said, Here am I..." (1 Samuel 3:2-5)

The only person Samuel knew would have been calling him was Eli. *"And the Lord called Samuel again the third time. And he arose and went to Eli, and said, Here am I; for thou didst call me. And Eli perceived that the Lord had called the child."* (1 Samuel 3:8) The first time the Lord called Samuel he ran to his mentor. The second time the Lord called Samuel, he ran to his mentor. The third time, the Lord called Samuel, Eli perceived, "Wait a minute, I'm in the house. Samuel is in the house. This is the Lord making the call." Notice, God did not come to Samuel in a voice that was different than the voice of his mentor. The voice of God will always sound like the voice of your mentor. Voice does not refer to the tone. It refers to the spirit of the revelation that your mentor shares.

Who Are You Sustaining?

"And the word of the Lord came unto him saying, Arise, get thee to Zarephath, which belongeth to Zidon, and dwell there: behold, I have commanded a widow woman there to sustain thee. So he arose and went to Zarephath. And when he came to the gate of the city, behold, the widow woman was there gathering sticks: and he called to her, and said, Fetch me, I pray thee, a little water in a vessel, that I may drink."
(1 Kings 17:8-10)

Now, Elijah went to Zarephath because a widow woman was already commanded to sustain him. Perhaps the widow woman was commanded to sustain the prophet, but she did not know it. Sometimes God will put a decree in your members that your intellect has yet to grab. In other words, before we came into the earth, Spirit impregnated each person with an assignment. However, many people have yet to understand their assignment. You probably didn't know what your assignment was when you were a year old. You probably didn't know what your assignment was when you were five years old. You may have even gone to school and taken numerous courses that were completely unrelated to your assignment (or so it appears). Nevertheless, you were pregnant with a mission when you got here. Think about it— You were already commanded before you operated in the command!

~

PRINCIPLE #29

*Who you sustain determines how you
are maintained.*

~

A widow woman was commanded to sustain the prophet. Who you sustain determines how you are maintained. If you are not sustaining the Master Prophet, you are not being maintained prophetically. If you are not sustaining your mentor or your leader, your life is not on God's maintenance program. Oftentimes, people miss their provision because they refuse to operate according to God's maintenance plan. God maintains you in accordance to your obedience to who He told you to sustain?

As the Son of the Prophet (the mentee), your ministry is not unto the Lord, as you may know the Lord, but your ministry is really unto a person (your mentor). Samuel ministered before Eli, yet he knew not the Lord. Eli was the priest. Samuel ministered in the temple. It was not until Eli was close to death that God started dealing with Samuel as a prophet. Joshua did not hear God's voice until Moses was dead.

God will never speak to the mentee until his mentor is dead. It is the Master Prophet's responsibility to point the mentee to the Lord, and it is the responsibility of the mentee to point the people to the Master Prophet. You may think that God has this intimate relationship with you; however, your relationship is really with your mentor. God and your mentor are inseparable. God and delegated authority are one. This is a vital principle to understand. When you understand that God and delegated authority are one, you will prophesy from the same dimension, that "I and my Father are one." You cannot proclaim, "I and my Father are one" if you see yourself separate from the Father. You can only see yourself separate from the Father if you are not in covenant with the Father or if you are not operating as one authority with the Father.

"Now the boy Samuel ministered to the Lord before Eli. The word of the Lord was rare and precious in those days. There was no frequent or widely spread vision. At that time, Eli, whose eyesight had dimmed so that he could not see, was lying down in his own place." (1 Samuel 3:1, Amplified Bible)

Sometimes God will cause you to minister before a half-blind priest to see whether you will be faithful to your assignment. But notice in Verse 7, *"Samuel did not yet know the Lord, and the word of the Lord was not yet revealed to him."* You can minister before the Lord and not know Him. Therefore, it is important to understand the aspects of authority.

God Speaks To Only One!

The Sons of the Prophet are praisers. It is the Son of the Prophet's responsibility to praise the Master Prophet, and it is the Master Prophet's responsibility to praise God. If you really study the scriptures, you will see that God did not speak to people individually. God really spoke to one person. God does not speak to every person individually concerning the corporate body. God speaks to one person, and then He looks to see if you can discern the person through whom He is speaking. God did not have conversations with Jesus' twelve disciples, nor did they wake up each morning with special revelation.

⌒

PRINCIPLE #30

God speaks to one person, and then He looks to see if you can discern the person through whom He is speaking.

⌒

However, in today's Church, many people come with their own agenda and their own purpose. The true prophet must ask himself, *"Who am I called to serve?"* He must declare within himself, *"I am called to serve my mentor. I am called to serve my leader. I am not here to build my own vision. I am here to build the vision of my mentor."*

Imagine the disciples saying to Jesus, *"Jesus, I heard something from the Father today that I need to tell you? While you were asleep, the Holy Spirit spoke to me. The Father had a word for the group today."* No! The disciples were there to serve the Master. On one occasion, Jesus even rebuked Peter, saying, *"Satan, the Lord rebuke you."* It was not the place of the disciples and the prophets to go to the Master and give directives. They were still in training. Therefore, if they gave directives, they were rebuked.

You should not go to your mentor with your own vision. Your vision must die so that the vision of your mentor can live. You are there to make sure that that the vision of your mentor lives and prospers. Therefore, your vision must die while your mentor's vision is resurrected. And in the fullness of time, after you have been faithful unto the Lord and unto the man or woman of God to whom you are assigned, God will cause others to help resurrect your vision.

Get On Your Post!

Although the disciples were with Jesus, they did not do any other ministry outside of the ministry that Jesus had given them. As the Son of the Prophet, you should be in church every Sunday because you are assigned to cover the leader. You are not there to preach. You are there to cover. You are the anointed cherub. The cherub was a covering angel. For example, your mentor may ask you to visit the sick. However, if you feel that you are too busy and you fail to visit the sick, then you are out of order. What is the problem? The problem is not that you didn't have time; the problem is you were not at your assigned post. If you are not on your post, you have uncovered the nakedness of your father.

~

PRINCIPLE #31

God is a God of order. If you miss the order,
you will miss God.

~

57

God is a God of order. If you miss the order, you will miss God. There are many individuals who thought they were ministering unto the Lord, only later to discover they have never ministered unto the Lord. It was just an illusion. Remember, your ministry is to your mentor. God will always assign you to a person unto whom you will minister. God will always assign you to cover a man.

> *God is a God of order. If you miss the order, you will miss God.*

Therefore, if you are not on your post in ministry, then you have uncovered your leader, and you have uncovered the Lord. Thus, you have not hidden your father's "nakedness." The Son of the Prophet must do everything he/she can to complete the assignment given by the Master Prophet. As a result of completing your assignment, your miracle and blessing will manifest. God will cover you because you covered the leader.

In ministry you will always be put to a test. You may have a report that is due for your job. Suddenly, your leader calls a five-night revival. You may say, *"Well, God gave me common sense."* You can either work by the laws of common sense or you can work by the laws of faith by operating under the grace of the leader. If you get under the grace of your leader, God will cover you because you covered Him. All of a sudden your boss will say, *"You don't have to do the report, but everyone else does."* Why? Because you were in place. You were on your post serving your leader, so God covered you.

You must remember that there is only **ONE** power. Although your boss is different than the person to whom you are spiritually assigned, if you have a belief in two powers, you will never see them as one in the same.

Ministry goes far beyond performing miracles, casting out devils, and/or having a strong prophetic anointing. Your mentor can teach you these aspects of ministry in a matter of minutes. Your mentor can teach you how to prophesy in less than two minutes, if you are willing to see. It is just a matter of opening up your third eye. It doesn't take much for you to speak; just say, *"Thus saith the Lord,"* and let it flow. It doesn't take much faith. The difficulty lies in understanding structure and authority and operating in order.

~

PRINCIPLE #32

Your mentor is the last face of God you will meet before you meet God Himself.

~

Many people believe that they are ministering to God, yet they have bypassed God altogether. How can you love God, whom you have not seen, and not love your brother, whom you have seen? The same principle applies in the mentor/mentee relationship. Your mentor is the last face of God you will meet before you meet God Himself.

The mentee must be the echo of his mentor. If your mentor is teaching on prosperity, then you are supposed to be teaching on prosperity. You should not be teaching on healing. You may say, *"Lord, I have this burning feeling. I know you want me to minister healing."* No! If your mentor is not teaching on healing, then you should <u>not</u> teach on healing. Jesus' disciples had no original thoughts. Likewise, the mentee

59

should not have any original thoughts. The only thoughts you are supposed to have are the thoughts of your mentor, and your mentor is getting his/her thoughts from God.

Your mentor knows where he is going. God has given him a vision and he knows how far to execute it. As the mentee, your are supposed to be the outstretched arm of your mentor. When people see you they see your mentor, because the mentee is the amplifier of his mentor's silence-life. The Master Prophet's life in silence becomes the Son of the Prophet's life demonstrated. As the mentee, you should demonstrate what your mentor has taught in silence. People should be able to pick up on the vibration. When someone comes to you with a problem, do they leave out of your presence saying, *"You sound like your leader"*? Are they able to distinguish between your voice and your mentor's voice? If they are able to distinguish your voice, then you have not completely died to self.

Your mentor will utter many truths in silence, and as the mentee, you are called to demonstrate these truths before the world publicly. Remember, you are the echo, and you must never to try to be the <u>voice</u>. There is a difference in <u>being</u> a voice and <u>giving</u> a voice. If you are a voice, you choose to be independent of your mentor. Make sure that when you give a voice it is an echo of your mentor.

Raise The Standards

"Let every soul be subject unto the higher powers. For there is no power but of God: the powers that be are ordained of God. Whosoever therefore resisteth the power, resisteth the ordinance of God: and they that

resist shall receive to themselves damnation. For rulers are not a terror to good works, but to the evil..." (Romans 13:1-3)

A ruler is a terror to evil work. If you fear your leader that may be a sign that there is evil in you, unresolved issues within yourself that you have not faced. These unresolved issues produce fear. For example, if you were driving on the highway doing the speed limit, you should not fear a police officer who is driving behind you. However, you may say to yourself, *"My lights are on. I have my license and registration."* You are almost waiting for them to stop and check you; you know you were doing the speed limit because you had the cruise control. You think to yourself, *"There is no way he can cite me for anything."* On the other hand, if you were speeding, you would have a problem with the officer stopping you. Now, you are fearful.

If you serve your mentor out of fear, it reveals that evil is in your heart. It exposes the intent.

~

PRINCIPLE #33

Your mentor is a terror to evil work.

~

"For rulers are not a terror to good work, but to evil. Wilt thou then not be afraid of the power? Do that which is good, and thou shalt have praise of the same. For he is the minister of God to thee for good..." (Romans 13: 3-4)

Every ruler is a minister of God. We serve so that we can do away with evil. We serve to become a terror to evil. We serve to reward good and to punish evil. However, we do not determine what is evil and what is good. Our service will highlight that within itself. Many times you will find that when you serve there will be people who will hate you for no reason at all; this comes with the package of ministry. If you are not willing to accept the package, then get out of ministry. Ministry requires that you go more than the extra mile, beyond the call of duty, beyond the realm in which you currently operate.

"...But if thou do that which is evil, be afraid; for he beareth not the sword in vain; for he is the minister of God, a revenger to execute wrath upon him that doeth evil." (Romans 13:4)

It is the minister's responsibility to execute wrath upon those who do evil, to execute wrath upon those things which are out of order, to execute wrath against those things that are not operating according to Divine law. The minister is called to execute the wrath of God. You have to be willing to execute the wrath of God and to minister judgments. How do you minister judgments? By having a standard.

Ministry demands order and adherence to protocol.

Ministry demands order and adherence to protocol. You must begin to make adjustments and rethink your reasons for being in ministry. You must move in the direction of accountability because you have responsibility for those who are under you. You have the responsibility before God for those upon whom you lay hands.

If you are not in tune with your emotions it will manifest in your life and in your experience. It will manifest in your home. It will manifest in the environment in which you live. If there is no structure in your home, if there is no structure in your closet, then there will be no structure in your life. If there is no structure in the way you place your shoes, there is no structure in your walk. If there is no order in your money, and your money is facing different directions in your wallet, then there will be no order in your finances.

In the Amplified Bible Romans 13:1 reads, "*Let every person be loyally subject to the governing civil authorities. For there is no power or no authority except from God by his permission, his sanction. And those that exist do so by God's appointment.*" There is a cross-reference in Proverbs 8:15, "*By me kings reign and rulers do decree justice.*"

There can be no king who reigns or no ruler who can decree justice unless God has ordained it to be so. The Amplified bible says in Romans 13:2, "*Therefore he who resists and sets himself up against the authority resists what God has appointed and arranged in divine order...*" When you are not in authority you are cutting the grain of the universal order. Oftentimes, you may not understand the judgments that the leader makes. However, it is not for you to understand; it is for you to remain under the covering of authority. The greater your submission to your leader, the greater your authority. You will not be able to demonstrate prophetically if you are not in divine order.

~

PRINCIPLE #34

You must be in divine order.

~

The pressure is getting under authority and staying there. Something is being formed. If you do not understand the judgment, you may become disillusioned. You may find yourself getting caught up in a moment instead of understanding the importance of the relationship. If you are not under authority or under the right covering, you are considered a "delirious mystic." A "delirious mystic" is someone who can see in the spirit, understand spiritual matters to a degree, but operates outside of order. If you are unable to point to visible authorities to whom you are supposed to be connected, the strength of your prophetic word is weakened, and you will find that the power is not there because you resist the powers that be.

"Therefore he that resists and set himself up against the authorities resists what God has appointed and arranged in divine order; and those who resist will bring down judgment upon themselves, receiving the penalty due them."(Romans 13:2)

God does not punish you. Evil does not come to you because God sends evil in your direction. Evil only comes to you because you order it to come in your direction. You must make sure you are in right behavior and right standing. However, a ruler is a terror to evil work. The prophet must be able to recognize authority. Otherwise, he may find himself going into a local church, not respecting or honoring the authority of that house, and then trying to give a prophetic word. It is important to understand the concept of authority, recognize authority and discern authority so that you don't prophesy on the wrong side of the fence.

Accountability And Submission

God is calling for accountability and order in the house of the Lord. The church is the support of truth. It is the pillar. It is the prop. These are the days where the Lord is exposing those who thought they had the heart of David, but are discovering in their generation that the heart of Saul is becoming more vivid in their lives each day. God is calling the "Hagars" that have run to the wilderness to escape the heavy hand of their mistress to come out of the wilderness, in spite of their grief, and return to their mistress and submit. *"And he went in unto Hagar, and she conceived: and when she saw that she had conceived her mistress was despised in her eyes."* (Genesis 16:4) This is the first time the word "mistress" is used in the Bible. In other words, it is time to stop running away from authority and run back into authority.

When you are under authority and become impregnated with a vision, you may find yourself feeling distressed because, in a sense, you are the mistress. The mistress is the one who is under authority and has conceived the vision. However, she will be despised by the one in authority because, for whatever reason, her season to birth her vision has not yet come. The prophet will always be faced with the challenge of, "Should I submit?" "Should I connect?" "Can I continue to remain?" However, his relationship must be tested, for it will reveal whether he is ready for the deeper dimensions of God.

Submission is not as much an outward expression, as it is a mindset and attitude of the heart. The heart of God is beating in this hour and drawing men and women of like spirit together. This is not a time to allow anything to disturb or remove the planting of the Lord.

~

PRINCIPLE #35

God and delegated authority are inseparable,
for there is no power but of God.

~

Do You Trust Me?

"And Sarai said unto Abram, My wrong be upon thee: I have given my maid into thy bosom; and she saw that she had conceived. I was despised in her eyes: the Lord judged between me and thee." (Genesis 16:5)

Many believers say, *"May the Lord watch between me and thee, while we are absent, one from another…"* However, this is a prayer of distrust. This prayer means that you believe the other person around you is a thief or a crook or a murderer. Why would the Lord need to watch if there is trust?

"And the angel of the Lord found her by a fountain of water in the wilderness, by the fountain in the way of Shur. And he said, Hagar, Sarai's maid, whence camest thou? and whither wilt thou go? And she said I flee from the face of my mistress Sarai. And the angel of the Lord said unto her, Return to thy mistress, and submit thyself under her hands." (Genesis 16:7-9)

Why would God command Hagar to submit under the hand of her mistress? Because her mistress' hand is the hand of God. The stress that her mistress is putting her under is going to help her perform the vision that she is carrying. Remember, God and delegated authority are inseparable.

You will always be faced with the challenge of submission. When you are ready for the deeper dimensions of God, your relationship with your mentor will be tested. Your relationship will always be tested to reveal how deep you are ready to go. Can you discern the many faces of God? If you take shortcuts, you will find yourself getting cut short. God does not make leaders. God makes servants, and the servants become the leaders. Therefore, you must stay covered. You cannot be in a ministry and have no covering. It is very important that the prophet be able to point to an overseer.

God will put you under men or women of God who will operate as seers over you, but you have to trust them. Usually, what they will ask of you will seem impossible. You will say, "I can't do that." However, your mentor hates your present body. Instead, he celebrates your future body (or your future self). He knows that you are destined to change. Your mentor is always projecting into your future. He has the responsibility of preparing you to morph into your future body.

～

PRINCIPLE #36

Your mentor hates your present body, he celebrates your future self.

～

Many people do not like what they have to morph into, but there must be a metamorphosis, and whenever there is a metamorphosis, you have to morph. You have to undergo internal reconstruction. When you begin to undergo internal reconstruction, your language will change. You will be forced to speak with a new tongue. Why? Because you are in a new body. The widow woman at Zarephath was speaking the tongue of starvation. However, she had to speak the tongue of the harvest. She was speaking the tongue of death. She had to speak the tongue of life. She was speaking the tongue of, "it's over." She had to speak the tongue of, "it's just beginning." She had to morph from one body to another.

If you do not undergo internal reconstruction, you will slowly die. The issues in you must be settled. There are many issues in you that will try to surface. However, the formation is going to change and you will have to begin to operate according to the "Law of Assumption" where you assume the next body. How ready are you to assume the next phase of your life? How ready are you to assume the role you are ordained to come into? God is asking, Can you go back and submit to your mistress? Can you assume that role so that I can make a great nation out of you?"

Your friends love you just the way you are. They don't want you to change. However, the moment you change, you will not have the same group of friends, unless they decide to change with you. Once you start to change your ideas will change. When your ideas change, your surroundings change. When your ideas change, the people that are around your life begin to change. When your ideas change, the people that are in your circle change, and you begin to reap a new destiny.

~

PRINCIPLE #37

How ready are you to assume the next phase of your life?

~

Your mentor is in your life to manipulate your mind. Your mentor changes your ideas so that you can reap a new destiny. However, this change must first start from deep within yourself. There are varying degrees of change that will take place. First example, physically, your hair changes color and your features change. Why? You are morphing into a different body.

You must constantly come into new thought. If you are not coming into new thought, then you are not morphing. Paul says, in Romans 12:2, *"Be not conformed to this world, but be ye transformed..."* How are you transformed? By the renewing of your mind. There can be no transformation until the mind has been renewed. The same thought (mind) that created the problem is not the same thought (mind) that can solve it.

A parent may say to your child, *"Okay, you created that mess; you solve it!"* However, do not expect him to solve the problem right away because he may be in the same mind that created the problem. Change must always take place. The first change has to take place in your language. When your language changes you will begin to see your lifestyle change and then the healing will begin.

Life is drawn from the source. Your mentor causes you to stay connected to the source. You cannot be in ministry and have no cover. When you do not have covering, you create certain problems. When you are not under authority, you cut against the grain of universal order, because everything in the universe submits. Night submits to day, and day submits to night. Everything in the universe is arranged in some kind of order.

The greater your submission, the greater the degree of your authority. You may not always understand the judgment of your leader. Nonetheless, you must remain under the cover of authority. If you do not submit under divine order, you will not be able to demonstrate prophetically. You can only demonstrate prophetically to the degree of the authority under which you submit and function. The difficult part is getting under authority and staying there. There will always be tests that challenge your level of submission. However, each test will bring you to a different level.

~

PRINCIPLE #38

When you are not under authority, you cut against the grain of universal order, everything in the universe submits.

~

Clearance For The Journey

Remember, if you do not have a mentor you will become a "delirious mystic." Psychics are delirious mystics, because they function independent of the church. They are not under spiritual authority. The Bible says that rebellion is as the sin of witchcraft. (1 Samuel 15:23) Witchcraft is not Tarot, astrology, herbs, necromancy, or tea leaf reading. In the scriptures people have done all of those things, and it was not considered witchcraft. Witchcraft is not the effect. It is not an act. If someone burns candles, it is not witchcraft. In the scriptures, the priests burned candles in the temple. So, burning candles cannot be witchcraft. It was considered witchcraft because they were not operating under authority.

You may say, "They were reading leaves in the cup. That's witchcraft!" But why do you think Joseph had the cup? What do you think Joseph was doing in Pharaoh's court as he was drinking and looking at the drinks in the cup? Why did they make such an issue about Joseph's cup? Joseph was probably using the cup to "divine." Don't let the word "divine" frighten you. He was trying to hear the mind of God for a situation for the king.

You may say "They are reading Tarot cards. That's witchcraft!" No. You may say, "Well, Astrology is definitely witchcraft." But why did Joseph have a dream of the 12 stars, the sun and the moon, and he knew the sun and moon represented his mother. The stars, the sun and the moon are astrological symbols. Christianity began as a result of a journey that the wise undertook based on a star.

You may say, "They talk to the dead. That's necromancy." But what do you think Jesus was doing when he was on the Mount of Transfiguration? Moses and Elijah were dead. However, Jesus was under authority. What is the difference? The difference is that these individuals were operating under authority. In other words, as a prophet, you have to make sure that you are under authority and that you have clearance to go in and access this information, because it is only available to those who are under authority.

E-MOTION

You must learn to master your emotions under authority. When you are not in tune with your emotions, it will manifest in your life and in your experience, because emotion create motion. The word "emotion" comes from the French word, *emouvoir*, meaning "to stir up" (from the Old French, *esmovoir*); from the Latin word, *emovere*, meaning "to remove; to displace."

When you respond according to your emotions, you displace something else (another feeling). An emotion replaces a present motion. If I start to laugh right now, that is an emotion, which means that I just displaced seriousness. Genesis 1:1 says, *"In the beginning, God created the heavens and the earth. And the earth was without form and void, and darkness was upon the face of the deep.* God creates everything out of nothingness ("no-thing-ness"). The earth existed in His mind, in His imagination, but He said, "We are not going to get the earth pressed out until I can have a motion about it. I have to make a motion." How do I make a motion? Have an emotion over it.

Until you can feel it, you cannot fill it. Until you can feel it and motion it out of you, there will not be any movement. Emotion allows the movement of thought into experience. After there was a movement of God (which meant God had feeling about it), then God said, *"Let there be light."* "Let light be on My feelings."

Whenever there is emotion happening within you, there is a physical reaction in your body. You may start to breathe heavy because the energy is building up, which produces something outwardly. Others will be able to detect your emotion. Emotions create motion. The motion that is within you creates the motion outside of you.

⌇

PRINCIPLE #39

Emotion creates motion.

⌇

I Made A Vow...

"But unto Hannah he gave a worthy portion; for he loved Hannah: but the Lord had shut up her womb. And her adversary also provoked her sore, for to make her fret, because the Lord had shut up her womb. And as he did so year by year, when she went up to the house of the Lord, so she provoked her; therefore she wept and did not eat. Then said Elkanah her husband to her, Hannah, why weepest thou? and why eatest thou not? And why is thy heart grieved? Am I not better to thee than ten sons? So Hannah rose up after they had eaten in Shiloh, and after they had drunk. Now Eli the priest sat upon a seat by a post of the temple of the Lord. And she was in bitterness of soul, and prayed unto the Lord, and wept sore. And she vowed a vow, and said, O LORD of hosts, if thou wilt indeed look on the affliction of thine handmaid, and remember me, and not forget thine handmaid, but wilt give unto thine handmaid a man child, then I will give him unto the LORD all the days of his life, and there shall no razor come upon his head. (1 Samuel 1:5-11)

Hannah's womb had been shut. But Hannah does something very interesting in Verse 11; she made a vow. We see here that the head (or the presider, or the Master Prophet) came forth, but he came forth because his mother vowed a vow. Hannah's womb was shut until she was able to come to a place of saying, "It's yours, Lord." Oftentimes we want things for us, but we don't want it for the Lord. When you understand prophetic anointings, it has to be brought to a place where it's all yours, Lord. It's no longer I, but the Christ.

Let's look at Hannah's actions prophetically. She vowed that no razor would come upon her son's head. Prophetically, Hannah was saying, "I don't want his thoughts to be cut or trimmed back." Hannah vowed a vow, and she asked the Lord to look upon her affliction. Hannah gave birth to a child and his name was Samuel.

Let's go back to 1 Kings 17:11-13:

"And she was going to fetch it, he called to her, and said, Bring me, I pray thee, a morsel of bread in thine hand. And she said, As the Lord thy God liveth, I have not a cake, but an handful of meal in a barrel, and a little oil in a cruse: and, behold, I am gathering two sticks, that I may go in and dress it for me and my son, that we may eat it, and die. And Elijah said unto her, Fear not, go and do as thou hast said: but make me thereof a little cake first, and bring it unto me, and after make for thee and for thy son."

This woman had thoughts of death. She was in a situation where her son was between starvation and death. She was down past her last. What do you do when you are down past your last? You give further. Notice what happened when Elijah spoke. Elijah threw the woman in deeper debt. I want to call that the "crisis of healing," to be thrown into a deeper dilemma in order to come forth with pleasant results. It is the pain of the cure.

Your mentor will throw you into a painful situation to see if you are moving in the law of trust. You cannot get the blessing of your mentor until you can trust your mentor. This takes the relationship of the mentor/mentee to another level. What is trusting your mentor? When you can turn off the lights in your world, walk blindly in the dark of your world, and trust that you will hold the hand of your mentor only. "It is no longer I, but it is the Christ." You lose your self-hood and begin to take on the life of your mentor.

You must go down past your last, then the only life you will have is the life of your mentor. God says, "I have to now throw you into the arena where you meet your end so I can begin." The prophet came into the widow woman's life for her head, not for her food. The prophet symbolizes the mind of God.

~

PRINCIPLE #40

Go down past your last.

~

Are you eating the head of your mentor? Are you eating the thoughts of your mentor? Are you eating the mind of the mentor? Elijah wanted the woman to feed off of his mind and not off of her last cake. Are you feeding off the mind of your mentor or the word of the Lord, or are you feeding off of your job, your income, your natural sustenance? Remember, your mentor is in your life to change your thinking. He changes your thoughts so he can change the destiny of your life. The prophet comes to change what is in your mind so he can change what will come into your hand.

The widow woman saw in her hand a handful of meal. She saw her last offering. However, the prophet saw beyond the offering. He saw that she was about to sow into the wrong place. She was about to sow her last into her dying son, which would not have resulted in her son being healed or his life spared. As a matter of fact, let me say something that may be very painful. She was literally feeding her son to death. She was feeding him death.

You could be working to death? You could be living to death. The only thing that has life is the word of the Lord in the prophet. The word of the Lord in the prophet becomes your life. 2 Chronicles 20:20 says, *"Believe in the Lord your God, so shall ye be established; believe his prophets, so shall ye prosper."* Your prosperity is in your belief in the prophet. If you don't believe in a prophet, there is no prosperity.

What is true prosperity? The widow woman's prosperity did not come to life until she believed the words of Elijah. "Give me the bread first. Feed my belly first." Then she started living. They just did not live for a day, but they lived for many years thereafter. However, Elijah had to first throw her into a crisis, the crisis of healing. Until the prophet throws you into a crisis, you have not had a visitation of God.

A crisis is very intense. It is that pivotal point in your life where you can win or lose, live or die. It is at that point where you will have to make a decision, a choice. The choice you make will determine whether you will live or die. The choice you make will determine whether you will be successful or unsuccessful. The choice you make will determine whether you will live in prosperity or live in poverty.

The word "crisis" comes from the Greek word, *krisis,* which literally means "decision; or to decide." The prophet forces you to make a decision, to be certain, to be settled. It is like he throws you into the wisdom of uncertainty, only to bring you back into another situation, which is a crisis.

For example, a midlife crisis can be very emotional, and results in a radical change of status in a person's life. A man may be in mid-life where he has to decide that he is no longer going to be a youth. If he does not make the right decision, it becomes a crisis because he is not growing. He is not moving forward. He is moving backwards in life. The 40-year old man wants to retreat to the 20-year old boy. This is a crisis. Why is it a crisis? He is being brought to a place where he has to decide, and he doesn't want to make the decision to be who he is ordained to be.

~

PRINCIPLE #41

*Until the prophet throws you into a crisis,
you have not had a visitation of God.*

~

The prophet forces you to be decisive. The prophet takes what appears to be stable, throws it into greater instability, and brings it into a crucial time in which a decisive change is impending. You can be in an environmental crisis whereby your whole environment becomes unstable, and the prophet will show up in your life to add more instability to it.

"I come here as a prophet; now there is an extra mouth to feed." "We are already unstable. You want to take the food out of my child's mouth?" "Yes! Because what you are feeding him is death, and I am saying, if you feed me it will become life. So, now you have to trust the prophet. I asked you for a whole cake, and you said, 'All I have is a handful of meal, and I'm going to give it to my son and we're going to die'" "Well, listen, before you kill your son, I need you to bury that last cake offering in me."

77

If the woman and her son ate the cake, it would have been death to them, but it was life to the prophet. The prophet has the ability to bring forth life because he is the life of God, the voice of God. Not only will it be life to the prophet, it will be life to the person that is giving it. It has to be buried in the prophet, to a point of no return. The prophet really comes to bring you into controversy, to bring you into a crisis?

The prophet comes into your life to throw you into a dilemma. If you have been drinking what you thought was orange juice for 20 years, and then someone later told you, "No, this is water," you would say, "This isn't water; it's orange juice." This is what you believed from the time you were born. Now you are in a crisis, because you have to come to a definitive point in a decisive moment. A crisis is a radical change that can get you in route to healing and wholeness.

Your mentor is your future self. The mentee is your past self. One stands before you as your future body; the other stands before you representing your past body. One represents what you were, the other represents what you shall be. Therefore, your mentor will inflict the greatest amount of pain in your life. All growth brings pain. As a child's physical body grows and matures, he will experience aches in his bones or growing pains. Why is their pain in growth? Because you have morphed from your old self to your new self. You have to start to shed off the old. Remember, the mind that created the problem is not the same mind that solves the problem.

~

PRINCIPLE #42

*A crisis is a radical change that can get you
in route to healing and wholeness.*

~

CHAPTER 5

THE ORPHAN

The Outcast

As I researched the scriptures, I discovered that the prophet-ic mantle was not passed down through the family like a dynasty. The priesthood was passed down from the father to the son; the kingship was passed down from the father to the son; but the prophetic mantle did not get passed down through the bloodline from a natural father to a son. Just because the father was a prophet and the grandfather was a prophet, did not necessarily mean that the son would be a prophet.

What I discovered is that the prophets are the orphans. The prophets are the outcasts of the group. Oftentimes, the prophets do not grow up and have the privilege of having things passed on to them. They do not walk in the shoes of their parents. The prophets are often rejected. They come out of obscure places. They walk through the wilderness. They have to be rejected by the tribe that they were born in so that they can begin to create a soul within themselves

79

and have the ability to do for themselves. Oftentimes, the prophet has to be kicked out of the group and forced to be an orphan so that he can become the prophet that God has ordained. The prophet has the potential to perform miracles, but as long as he is kept, he will not perform.

For example, when we look through the scriptures, we see the call of the prophet Elisha. Elisha had to leave his father and mother in order to become a son of the prophet. The prophet Samuel was given up for adoption. In the same way, you may have been raised by someone other than your birth parents. You may have been an outcast in your family and never really understood the reasoning behind the rejection. However, the rejection is a direct relationship to the prophetic call on your life. You may have tried to reject this vocation so that you could gain the acceptance of the "tribe". Some people even rejected their vocation for the acceptance of a tribal relationship with which they were not in covenant.

However, when God creates a prophet He somehow pushes him out of his tribe. God pushes him away from his family and from those whom he is familiar. When Hannah gave birth to a prophet she realized that she could not raise him, so she had to turn him over to Eli.

~

PRINCIPLE #43

Prophets are the outcasts of the group.

~

As the orphan, the prophet is oftentimes considered strange. There may be whispers behind their backs concerning their aloofness. There is controversy surrounding how they ended up where they are. However, if they really understood their calling, they would dry the tears from their eyes and start walking with pride and dignity, because they would realize that they are a part of a prophetic community. Prophetic people will never be understood.

The individuals who see miracles in their lives are those who take responsibility for their destiny. They take control of their life and begin to walk in alignment with their destiny. They do not get sidetracked, but continue in the truth and demonstrate the truth in every area of their lives.

The prophet is oftentimes forced to be an orphan because he has to learn responsibility. He has to learn self-acceptance. He has to learn how to take care of himself. He has to learn how to feed himself. A prophet who depends on someone else to feed him will not be effective, because eventually he will walk away from being the prophet and become the prostitute. A prostitute is a person who does a task for the love of money. The prostitute can be a woman who stays in a marriage for security; she is there on the wrong terms. The prostitute can be a man who cannot leave his job when God unctions him to leave because he worries about how he will pay his bills.

The prostitute is really not wicked. She performs her service for survival. Therefore, if you are doing what you are doing for survival, you are not the prophet, you are the prostitute. There will come a time in your life when God will test whether you are the prophet or the prostitute.

The prophet knows rejection because the soul of the group rejects him. He is into the tribe, but he is not part of the tribe. He does not speak the same language as the tribe.

The tribe sees snow, the prophet sees clouds. As a result, he will sometimes be labeled the witch, because the group does not understand him, and consequently, he ends up being cast out of the group, though aligned with the group, because he sees things from a different dimension.

~

PRINCIPLE #44

Are you the prophet or the prostitute?

~

Don't Sell Your Birthright

The prophet's training is much different than the training of the tribe, because in the end, he may have to become the savior of the group by the prophetic word that he gives to the group. For example, Moses had to be taken out of his household and trained under another order. As the prophet, you have to accept the rejection because the rejection reveals your calling. Don't sell your birthright.

You may want to live close to your family member. However, the moment you want to live close to your family, your calling will pull you away. God may even cause an incident to erupt in your family just to keep you separated from the tribe. At one point in His ministry, Jesus asked the question, "Who is my mother?" Jesus responded, "They that do the will of my Father." (Matthew 12:48-50) Only a prophet can say, "Who is my mother?" "Who is my brother?" "Who is my sister?" The prophet sees relationship only in those who are in the will of God.

Joseph was kicked out of His tribal group. David was taken out and put at the table of Saul, and then kicked out by the soul of that group after he killed Goliath. When you read about Shadrach, Meshach, and Abednego, there is no mention of their parents either. When you have a prophetic calling on your life your parents may not be in the picture, because the calling is greater than your parents and the family into which you were born. In the end, you may go back and deliver them and bring salvation to them. However, as long as you are with them you cannot save them, because they are unable to equip you with the skills that you will need to operate in your calling. You must go out and get it for yourself.

It is only when you can accept being the orphan that you will discover your hidden power. As long as you have your mother and father to assist you, you will operate in their power. However, the moment you look over one shoulder and your mother is gone, and you look over the other shoulder and your father is gone, you will understand that you are called to the prophetic. "*When my father and mother forsake me, then the Lord will take me up.*" (Psalm 27:10)

Before you came to earth you entered into a covenant with your mother and father. God said to you, just like He said to Jeremiah, "I ordained you to be a prophet to the nations." Your mother and father knew that you were ordained to be a prophet to the nations. So, when God ordained you to be a prophet to the nations, part of the process was the rejection by your mother and your father. However, you, your mother and your father forgot the agreement that you made before you left heaven. You are walking the earth with amnesia, not remembering that you are in a covenant agreement. The rejection by your mother and your father is really a calling into the acceptance of the prophetic.

Oftentimes, God does not let the parents of a prophet raise the prophet. You may be crying and going through emotional changes trying to make family relationships work, and wondering why there is so much family dysfunction? It is your vocation; it is your calling, Prophet! It is your vocation; it is your calling, Prophetess! You may say, "I don't understand why my mother does all of this for her other children, but she has never done this for me." You are the prophet! "They gave everybody else something, but they have never given me anything." You are the Prophetess. Your inheritance comes from the Lord. You are supposed to produce your effects from within!

∼

PRINCIPLE #45

The prophet must produce his effects from within.

∼

As the prophet, you are supposed to be the subject of conversation in your community. There is supposed to be a conspiracy about your aloofness. There is supposed to be a controversial story about why you ended up where you are. There are supposed to be whispers behind your back. There are supposed to be people talking about you and talking against you. No one is supposed to be reaching their hand around the corner and putting a little something extra in your bank account. Why? You are prophetic! You are supposed to produce your effects from within! You may say, "They did this for this one, they did this for that one, and then when they got to me all of the money ran out." You are a prophet. Your calling created it. You are supposed to produce your effects from within!

The Prophet Amos said, *"I was no prophet, neither was I a prophet's son...and the Lord said unto me, Go, prophesy unto my people Israel,"* and Amos began prophesying. (Amos 7:14-15) When you are prophetic in nature and prophetic in temperament, as you look back over your life it sounds like you need a therapist. People can list all of the things you did wrong. You got pregnant before you were supposed to get pregnant. People may say, "This child has been a problem since the second grade." You were just creating one situation after the other. However, you are a prophet!

When you start to understand the ways of the prophet, prophetic people, and the prophetic calling, you will realize that your life is not the norm.

God speaks to the prophet. He will say, "Go do this." What is God doing? He is getting your attention. Every time God wants to get the prophet's attention, He will have the prophet do something that seems very strange to those around him. For example, the prophet Ezekiel was working with cow's dung. (Ezekiel 4:12) In another instance, Ezekiel slept on the left side so many nights and on the right side another time. He shaved his head bald and threw one third of his hair into the fire, one third into the water, and one third into the wind to prophesy concerning the state of Israel. (Ezekiel 5:1-5)

When you start to understand the ways of the prophet, prophetic people, and the prophetic calling, you will realize that your life is not the norm. As the orphan you have to learn to take responsibility for yourself. You have to take responsibility for your actions. You don't want to be the immature orphan, because then you will become the victim or the beggar. You want to be the mature orphan, operating in wisdom because you have learned how to take responsibility for your life. The mature orphan is not looking to be kept. He looks to produce his effects from within!

The prophet survives by his intuition and prophetic ability, not by natural knowledge. His gift has to feed his ability to discern the harvest, to discern the way of the Lord, to discern where the hand of God is moving, to discern which way God is shifting. You can only learn that as the orphan. If you have been starving long enough you know how to feed yourself intuitively from within. Can you work a miracle now?

Many times God will cut off the prophet's source. When you have to become a deliverer for a people, when you're going to bring a people out, your source will be eliminated.

∽

PRINCIPLE #46

The greater your rejection, the greater your anointing.

∽

Paul said, "The stone which the builders have rejected has become the chief cornerstone." (Mark 12:10) The greater your rejection, the greater your anointing. The prophet always has a story behind his birth or a scandal in the upbringing. The Bible says, *"When father and mother forsake me, the Lord will take me up."* The prophet has to be taken up in order to hear the voice of the Lord.

When you walk in the prophetic order it is often difficult to identify your parents because your orders are different, because when you give the word of the Lord, they cannot be on the sidelines stands saying, "Come here child, what did you say to them?" Therefore, God, in His sovereignty, has to cut the connection. He has to cut the umbilical cord. He has to cut what you come through. You come through your parents, but not from them. Your whole identity has to change in order for you to be a prophet.

Notice what God said to Jeremiah, *"Before I formed thee in the belly I knew thee; and before thou camest forth out of the womb I sanctified thee, and ordained thee a prophet unto the nations."* (Jeremiah 1:5) Your life as a prophet begins from eternity past. God never said He ordained you as a king before you were born. He never said he ordained you as a priest. Only prophets get the ordination papers before they get here.

When you become dependent on your mother and father, and they are unable to release you to become the orphan that you are supposed to be, where you trust only in Almighty God. Therefore, God will do a circumcision and cut them out of your life. The prophet has to become self-sufficient, so that no one can take the credit for his greatness, only Almighty God.

Therefore, when you pray prayers like, "Lord, I want my child to be a prophet," know that you have just signed the death certificate in your relationship. The prophet has to leave the tribe to save the tribe, because you can't save the tribe with the same mind that is in the tribe. The prophet has to be dependent on God and God alone.

In the scriptures, Jesus never refers to his mother as "mother." He calls her "woman." He already divorced her as mother. If He had always seen her as "mother," His prophetic judgment may have been clouded. He may have become so tied to earth that he couldn't get a word from heaven.

The sooner the prophet can get into the earth and become the orphan, the sooner he can enter into his experience of knowing God, and then eventually find a mentor intuitively who will begin to lead and guide him and bring him into the truth that is ordained for his life.

~

PRINCIPLE #47

The prophet must be dependent on God and God alone.

~

The Wounded Child

The Bible says, *"...it pleased the Father to bruise him..."* (Isaiah 53:10) When you have a prophetic call on your life, it pleases the Father to bruise you. When you are bruised you are sensitive and you can hear clearly; you can feel clearly; you know when something brushes up against you. However, you cannot have feeling and sensitivity if there has not been a wound in your life. So, it pleases the Father to bruise you so that you can become sensitive to the move of the Spirit. It is the call of the prophet. Jesus was hanging on the cross as the "wounded child." Why? Because Jesus was a Prophet. Jesus was Prophet, Priest, and King. However, the bruise came because Jesus was a Prophet.

What is the difference between the "mature prophet" and the "immature prophet"? The "immature prophet" carries his wounds and never moves in the strength of his ministry. He walks the earth as a "wounded child" instead of as a sensitive soul to the mind of the Spirit. The "wounded child" is hurt and continues to nurture his pain until he nurtures himself into a victim mentality, feeling like everyone is against him. The "wounded child" develops into the wounded prophet and ministers from his wounds. For example, the wounded prophet may say, "Oh, yes, in 1977, she cursed me out. I'll never forget. It was a Friday night at 10:22." That is a wound. You must learn how to grow beyond that experience.

The wounded child is usually the second born. He picks up the emotions of the mother. The second born is usually the one who is wounded and has no voice, but wants to act out loud what mother has been called to suppress. The first-born, on the other hand, represents the father and wants to be the hero.

The wounded child is the individual who will probably carry the pain of the family. Jesus Christ was the second member of the Godhead. He was the one who was wounded. Abraham had two sons. The second son put a knife to him. We see Esau and Jacob, which one ran away? The second born. We see Cain and Abel, which one was slain? The second born. The second born is the one who carries the wound because they have to be brought to a place where they become the outcast of the group so that they can feel the rejection and absorb it.

The mature prophet, on the other hand, can take a licking and keep on ticking. Why don't you stop saying everyone is against you, and say it is part of your process and part of your calling. It is your training.

The Bible says, *"He was wounded for my transgressions, bruised for my iniquity. And the chastisement of my peace was upon him."* (Isaiah 53:5) But by every one of those wounds we as a people will be healed. What have you been carrying? What do you feel like you were left out of? What events happened in your life of which you are not proud? Know that those very stripes are healing those that you can feel. You cannot heal what you do not feel.

~

PRINCIPLE #48

When you have a prophetic call on your life,
it pleases the father to bruise you.

~

CHAPTER 6

PROPHETIC TIMING

—⊷ ⊠⊀⊠ ⊶—

"To everything there is a season, and a time to every purpose under the heaven." (Ecclesiastes 3:1)

What Time Is It?

Prophetic timing is God's timing. God is concerned about time. He is the greatest timekeeper the world has ever seen. God does whatever He wants to do in His own timing. He sets up a nation and puts another nation down. He promotes one person, and causes another person to lose his job. Therefore, when God begins to move in His timing we cannot say, "Lord, hold the clock. I am not ready yet. I need more time." When it's God's timing, you have to move whether you like it or not. Why? Because God is orchestrating and demonstrating His will and His purpose in the earth.

Are you operating according to God's timetable or have you fallen behind schedule? Are you perhaps running ahead of God? What time are you moving in? Or are you doing some work that you were supposed to do ten years ago? Are you playing catch up? Or are you trying to be God's wonder overnight? What time is it?

If you are called by God and you plan to operate according to His divine favor, then you must first operate in accordance with the time and the season that you are in. Ecclesiastes 3:2 says that there is a time to be born, and a time to die. There is a time to be born, to come forth in this earth, and there is a time to die. God uses His prophets to teach people how to live. Oftentimes people get so caught up with what is happening in their present, and what is going to happen in their future. However, what is happening in between? How are you living? What are you doing with your days?

Psalm 90:12 says, *"So teach us to number our days, that we may apply our hearts unto wisdom."* The Hebrew word "days" is *manah*, which means "to weigh out; to allot; to enroll; to appoint; to count; to set." We have a set time in God. Psalm 103:15 says, *"As for man, his days are as grass: as a flower of the field, so he flourisheth."* In this passage of scripture, the Hebrew word for "days" is *yome*, meaning from sunrise to sunset. It is a process of time. What process of time are you living in? Never let it be said that you started out good, but you stopped along the way. Never let it be said that you weren't able to fulfill and complete the work that God has given you.

∼

PRINCIPLE #49

There is a time for every purpose under heaven.

∼

God started a good work with the Children of Israel. He led them by His own hand, as a cloud by day and a fire by night. However, something occurred in the process. They continually looked back, murmured and complained and as a result missed their day of visitation. God has given each and every one of us a limited portion of time in which to work. How you choose to work your time is up to you. In this hour, God is asking what are you going to do with your time?

Prophetic timing is God's timing. Are you operating in God's timing? You don't want to miss the move of God. You don't want to miss the prophetic destiny that He has set before you. You don't want to miss your day of visitation. The race is not given to the swift, but it is given to those who endure to the very end. However, you have to continually have an open ear to hear what God is saying.

Jesus said, *"I must work the works of Him that sent me, while it is day: the night cometh, when no man can work."* (John 9:4) Jesus understood the principle of working while it was day. Everyone experiences night seasons in their lives. Therefore, it is vital that we do the work while it is day, in the right season, which is the prophetic timing of God. We cannot afford to miss out on what God wants us to do. Many people have died with their dreams, goals and aspirations never being realized because they thought they had more time. Many were afraid to tackle the projects that the Lord set before them. Fear grappled their hearts and caused them to be paralyzed before ever taking the first step. They never understood the importance of working while it was day. They never understood the seasons of God.

So, what is happening in this season? What is the Spirit uttering? We are standing at the door of a new age. God is looking for those who will walk in the light and help others who need to know this truth. There will be many people who will help others discover the genius within that the world has mislabeled. However, those people must understand the ages. You have to ensure that you are in your right season. Are you giving birth to an age?

Herod tried to kill an age. He said to the wise men, *"Go and search diligently for the young child; and when ye have found him, bring me word again, that I may come and worship him also."* (Matthew 2:8) But the angel told the wise men not to return to Herod, but to go back another way. Are you giving birth to an age or are you aborting an age. Many people are still trying to operate by the old rules, but the old rules will not work with this new generation. We are in an age where God is raising up deliverers.

Consider Joseph and his descent. Now, consider Nelson Mandela, whom God allowed to do something greater than Joseph. Joseph went from the prison to being Prime Minister. Mandela went from the prison to being President of his country. *"The glory of the latter house is going to be greater than that of the former."* (Haggai 2:9)

~

PRINCIPLE #50

Do not miss your day of visitation.

~

The prophetic dimensions of God reveal that we are in a season where there is a crossover between the Piscean and the Aquarian Ages. Some people are Piscean parents trying to raise an Aquarian child. They are lost, because they are still trying to "believe" and their children "know." They are hoping, and their children are growing. Their children are coming to teach them wisdom.

Jesus looked at his parents and he left. Jesus was lost for three to four days. When he returned, his parents said, "Where were you?" Jesus replied, "Don't you know? I was about my Father's business." He was operating from a realm that they didn't understand. The Bible says, He became "subject unto them." (Luke 2:41-52) This is the key for those people who have children who are geniuses. You have to train them to discern God in authority enough to be subject, because you can have a gift without wisdom. To have a gift without wisdom is disaster, because it is a gift that is not guided. If the gift is not guided, it is not guarded.

Today's generation will bring about an evolution to the world.

Today's generation will bring about an evolution to the world. They are bringing light to the world. This is an age of consciousness. It is an age of intellect. Information is circling in the air and is passing through you at all times; however, many people are not aware of it. You must have awareness and a keen understanding so that you can download the information that pertains to you. The prophets in this Age are going to be able to pick up on vibrations. They will know things through a level of intelligence that is not understood by the natural mind.

We are in an age of thinkers. We are in an age of winners. We are in an age where losers are moving out of the way and winners are on the horizon. We are in an age of persistence, an age where people know no boundaries, an age where people are not excited about being grounded, but where many people are saying, "I want to take off. It is boring down here. Let's get up." We are in an age where people have to seek out other arenas to find spirituality because the Church is still stuck in the "Stone Age" and cannot help them.

God said, *"In the last days I shall pour out my Spirit upon all flesh..."* He said, *"...and your sons and your daughters shall prophesy, and your young men shall see visions, and your old men shall dream dreams..."* (Acts 2:17) All flesh will be touched by the glory of God. The "old man" is not an old man defined by physical age. The "old man" is your Spirit man, the Ancient of Days, God in you who has dreamed the dream, and you are the "young man" manifesting? Are you doing the vision?

Grow Up!

Timing is essential to God's purpose. It is vital for every believer to understand the move of God. If you fail to understand God's move in your life, then you will continually operate as a baby, needing to be bottle fed. Jesus came and finished the work, and He was able to say at the end of His journey, *"It is finished."* (John 19:30) And God was able to say, *"This is my beloved Son, in whom I am well pleased."* (Matt. 3:17) Many people who profess to be mature in God have to be bottle fed. However, God is saying, come off the bottle. It is time for the meat of the word. You cannot live and be sustained by drinking milk only. You need a balanced diet.

God's desire is for His people to have a balanced diet. They must begin to eat the meat of God's Word. However, the meat is going to force you to chew. It will cause you to seek God for yourself and ask, "Lord, what will you have for me to do?" Your desire must be to fulfill the plan of God for your life in the land of the living. Jesus said in Luke 2:49, *"I must be about my Father's business."*

You must be about the Father's business. You must begin to prepare and plan now, so that you will know what you are going to do for the Lord in the earth. If you fail to plan, you plan to fail. It is imperative that you plan. Don't get caught in the trap of procrastination. Many believers say, "I'm going to let the Lord lead me." But this is a trap. It is an excuse to put off until tomorrow what God has told you to do today. God prepared the Last Supper thousands of years before it happened. God prepared the Lamb for us to come and die for our sins thousands of years in advance. Do you know your God's timetable for your life?

The right timing will produce life. Esther is the proof of this. When Esther went before the king, she used proper timing and prepared herself. She went before God asking for direction. She went to her covering (Mordecai) saying, "How should I do this?" And she received wise counsel enabling her to go forth and execute the plan of God properly. (See the Book of Esther)

You must move in your prophetic word according to the right timing, according to the timing that the Lord has given. That is the power of prophecy! You can receive a right word, but the timing may be off. If our timing is off, we can do more damage than good. Before a surgeon operates, he must prepare for the operation. If his preparation is incorrect, then the results can be hazardous and even deadly.

In the same way, we cannot execute one of God's operations in our lives without first preparing. We need the correct preparation so that the outcome will live. Whatever you do, move in accordance with God's timing and His agenda. If you hear "Green light, go," then move. However, if you hear, "Red light, stay," then DO NOT MOVE!

Don't Waste My Time

Many people have a tendency to waste time during their day, attributing it to "waiting on God." However, God never wastes time. We must see timing as an appointment. You have a scheduled event in your life that is orchestrated by God. You cannot afford to miss your appointment with God, your date with destiny. What has God said to you? What has He spoken in your innermost being? Are you moving left when God told you to move right?

We cannot have the 'Martha" spirit. Martha was busy doing a good work serving Jesus. However, her busyness kept her from doing what God wanted her to do, which was to sit at His feet and learn and enjoy His presence. Don't allow your busyness to take so much control of your life that you lose sight of the better things in life, which is sitting in the presence of God and hearing what He has to say to you. The devil does not care how busy you are. His desire is to get you away from the presence of God. Never become so busy that you are too busy to hear from God.

Therefore, take time to hear from the prophets of God who can reveal the mind of God to you in your life. It is vital to your survival in the earth, and vital to your productivity in Him. That is the Power of Prophecy! The prophetic word will shift you into the right timing of God and cause you to do great exploits for Him.

It's time for you to release the things that you have been holding. It is your time to go forth and begin to move in the prophetic word that God has given unto you. When it is your time nothing or no one can stop you. No one but **YOU** can detour you from your purpose. God seeks to revel Himself through you. When man says No! God says, Yes! When men turn their backs on you, God turns His face towards you and says, "Rise up, man or woman of God; Rise up! When man says you are weak, God says you are strong. When you feel you are insufficient and cannot do anything, God will encourage you and let you know that you can do all things!

See God moving in your life! See God motivating you to another level in Him. Allow the power of the prophetic word to move you into Divine order with God. Allow the power of the prophetic word to introduce you to your date with destiny! What time is it? It is time to rise up and be about your Father's business, for it is your time now!

Life is short, yet valuable. You must learn to savor every moment, because we never know when God will say, "It is finished." God only raises up winners! Seize the moment! **NOW** is the time! **NOW** is the acceptable year of the Lord! **NOW** is the time that God is calling you to walk in boldness for Him!

Time exists in the present, but it speaks to your future. What are you going to do in your future? If you are not doing anything in your present, chances are you will not do anything in your future. Time has a way of propelling you into your future. What time is it?

Proper timing can bring peace to every storm. That's God's timing! That is the Power of Prophecy! If you understand timing, you can slay the giants in your life. David knew it was his time. Neither Saul nor the other kings could slay Goliath. It wasn't their time. They looked the part, but it wasn't their time. David, though very young, had to be himself and move in what God told him to do. David moved in God's timing and was able to slay the giant!

~

PRINCIPLE #51

Proper timing will bring peace to any storm.

~

God has uniquely patterned you for His purpose. When it is your time, you have to move according to the way God has formed and fashioned you. You can't move the way someone else moves. You must move the way God has ordained for you to move. When you move according to God's timing, you will be able to go forth and slay every one of the giants in your life. God will give you the victory. He will show you how to do it.

Improper timing can defer your destiny. Many people have missed their purpose because they do not rightfully discern the timing of God. Every obedient act brings you closer to fulfilling God's plan. You have a choice. The scales are being weighed. Will you be obedient or disobedient to the Word of God?

Time is a commodity. You can spend it, waste it or invest it. It is very vital and very precious, and we must savor it by taking each moment as it comes. Don't let things and people cause you to miss your day of visitation. Don't let your children, your husband, your job, your church, your fears, and your cares or even YOU allow you to miss your day of visitation. The way you operate in your season of visitation will determine how you will deal with your future events, for your past is a prophecy of your present and future.

The Spirit world is timeless. When you begin to enter into the Spirit realm, time ceases. If you've ever had a visitation from God, walked with Him, or just spent time with Him, it is like hours. The scripture says that one day with the Lord is like a thousand years. (2 Peter 3:8) In the realm of the Spirit, the prophet can see your past, present and future happening all at the same time. The only way you will begin to see this happening is if you launch out into the deep, which is the realm of the Spirit. If you want to know where God is taking you, if you need to understand why you do the things that you do, then you must go into the realm of the Spirit and allow God to show you yourself.

God will show you what happened to your ancestors, and He will even show you what happened to you while you were in your mother's womb. God will take you back, but you have to apply yourself. You have to want it, and God will reveal it to you. Many people wonder why they are in a state of stagnation. "Lord, why isn't anything happening?" Why is everything I put my hands to not working?" I dare you to go before God and begin to ask Him some things. He will show you yourself. That is the Power of Prophecy!

Let go and let God. Let go of your old thinking. Let go of your traditions and the things that you thought God said to you. You have to desire fresh manna. You have to desire a fresh word from the Lord. Is there a word from the Lord? Yes, there is! All you have to do is reach up and grab it, because it is yours for the asking. God said there is no good thing that He will withhold from us if we just ask. Ask and He will give you what you need! That is the Power of Prophecy!

Let it not be said that you missed your visitation! Wake up and hear ye the Word of the Lord. Wake up out of your slumber and know that God is speaking to you! Wake up and see that God is on the move! That is the Power of Prophecy!

What time is it? It's God's time to let God move in your life!

~

PRINCIPLE #52

Let go and let god!

~

CHAPTER 7

THE PROPHETIC ALCHEMIST

⊷ ⊯⊹⊵ ⊶

Prophetic Symbolism

The physical body is really just a chemistry lab. There are four elements that are essential in every lab (body), earth, air, fire, and water. The physical body is seen as the earth. The Bible says, *"Let thy will be done in earth* (which means in us), *as it is in heaven"* (as it is in thought or our imagination). Air passes through the nostrils. God breathed into man's nostrils the breath of life (air), and man became a living soul. Man became the breath that was breathed into Him. The Word is the breath of life. The body must maintain a certain temperature (fire); and the body is made up of 80% water.

Understanding the mind of Christ allows you to better understand the elements that are essential in your laboratory (body) as you begin to create and speak as a prophet of God.

103

You will understand the breath of God. You will understand the fire, which is there to consume whatever is not God. (Only God can walk in the flames of the fire and not be consumed.)

"And the angel of the LORD appeared unto him in a flame of fire out of the midst of a bush: and he looked, and, behold, the bush burned with fire, and the bush [was] not consumed." (Exodus 3:2)

The miracle of the burning bush was that the bush was on fire, but it was not consumed. The prophet is supposed to be able to walk through the fire and not be consumed. You are walking in God, but you can still be seen. You are not consumed; you must be God.

Psalm 82.6 says, *"I have said, Ye are gods; and all of you are children of the Most High."* The word of the Lord is for you to come forth as Divinity. This is the hour where God is revealing His truths to His prophets. Therefore, the prophets must assume the responsibility of being the prophetic people that God has ordained. When you understand that the word of the Lord is for you to come forth, you are going to come forth as Divinity.

∽

PRINCIPLE #53

You must recognize the signature of God in everything around you.

∽

Fairytales and myths contain within them a degree of truth that oftentimes goes unrecognized. They contain a prophetic language of which many people are not aware.

This language is known as "prophetic symbolism." Timeless truths are stuck in simple stories. As prophets, it is vital that we begin to <u>see</u> the symbolism in everything that we touch, and start to <u>feel</u> the symbolism in everything around us. You must understand how to see and feel the symbols and recognize the signature of God in everything around you.

For example, during the Christmas Season the pulpit may be adorned with items that depict the Christmas holidays. Cotton may be used to represent snow; pine trees may be used to represent a Christmas tree; etc. One person may see the cotton on the pulpit and see it as just cotton. Someone else may see the cotton as representative of "clouds or snow." However, when the prophet sees the cotton, he can begin to break down the prophetic symbolism of the cotton. The cotton represents emotion. Clouds symbolize a Neptunian effect, the inability to see clearly through a situation. Water also represents a Neptunian effect. For example, let's look at Jonah. Because of Jonah's disobedience, he ended up in the belly of a big fish. He ended up in a place of uncertainty. He was in a dark night of his soul. You can't get more Piscean than that.

Usually, when you are in a season of disobedience, you will be in a place of cloudiness, a day of great uncertainty, until you say, yes, unless you have an inward navigation system. When you are in a season of uncertainty, when the navigation system has been shut down and the clouds are all around you that can be very Neptunian. "Should I walk to my right, should I walk to my left, should I go straight ahead, or should I walk backwards?" However, an inward navigation system will allow you to walk through the seasons of uncertainty in your life.

As the Prophet, you may walk through seasons of darkness, but you have an inward navigation system. Those around you may see darkness, but inwardly you have a knowing. That is why God had to take us from the age of believing into the age of knowing. Once you know who you are, you will come into that season of knowing.

Let's go back to the pulpit adorned with Christmas decorations. One person may see a pine tree as representative of a Christmas tree. The prophet looks at the pine tree and sees that it is not just a pine tree, but it represents earth. The prophet sees earth planted in water. Earth represents foundation. Earth brings structure.

So, what we really see on this stage is not a pine tree in snow, but the snow represents water, and the pine tree represents wood. The snow represents emotion, and the pine tree represents structure coming up out of emotion. So, to the prophet the scene actually depicts that a person has to know how to handle his/her emotions and out of it allow structure to emerge.

~

PRINCIPLE #54

*An inward navigation system will allow you to
walk through the seasons of uncertainty in your life.*

~

The Alchemist

*"Know ye not that you are the temple of the living
God."* (1 Corinthians 3:16)

The prophet has the ability to go within his chemistry lab (into his temple; within himself) to do the prophetic work of handling mysteries and turning thoughts into things. By shifting things with our eyes, we are able to change that which is base to that which is valuable in the twinkling of an eye. Despite the challenges, the prophet realizes that the ability to do this work is vital to saving the tribe. This dynamic teaching will prepare us for the coming age of knowing God and will cause the way of the prophetic alchemist to have global impact.

The alchemist is "all-chemistry," one who knows how to turn base metals into gold. The prophetic alchemist is the prophet who knows how to go into his prophetic laboratory within and create. If you do not understand how to create from your internal laboratory, you will not get the kind of results that you need to experience in life.

As the prophetic alchemist, we learn how to go within the chemistry lab. The chemistry lab is our temple. The Bible says, *"Know ye not that you are the temple of the living God."* You must go into your temple (your prophetic lab) so that you can do the prophetic work of handling the mysteries of God and turning thoughts into things (turn your water into ice). The way of the prophet is the way of the alchemist.

Religion places things in the far future. It disconnects people from reality and causes them to get caught up in the illusion. However, there comes a point when you must grow out of the mystery, out of that which is unseen, into that which is seen. You have to become that which does not appear, and begin to appear. Everything in life has a mystery. Therefore, you must go within so you can learn how to turn thoughts into things.

Your thoughts are very valuable because what you think you become. You are the sum total of your thoughts. It is very important that you are aware of what information your mind is bringing to you. Sometimes your mind can act as an "unruly disciple" and start to step out of line, like Peter did. In scripture, the disciples represent psychological thoughts that occasionally go through your mind. So, like Jesus, every now and then you may have to tell one of your thoughts, "Get thee behind me, Satan."

~

PRINCIPLE #55

You are the sum total of your thoughts.

~

There are times when you will have to go beyond your thinking, because your intellect will seek to become a barrier in the relationship between you and your Master. "Why did the Master say that?" "Why is he doing this?" "Why is he doing that?" Be careful of what your thoughts are bringing to you. If your thoughts are not echoing what the Master is saying, treat them like Peter and tell them to get behind you.

> *"Wherefore seeing we also are compassed about with so great a cloud of witnesses, let us lay aside every weight, and the sin which doth so easily beset [us],and let us run with patience the race that is set before us."* (Hebrews 12:1)

An alchemist is one who knows how to turn base metals into gold. Many people do not get a lift in life because they have too much base metal within them that they refuse to turn into gold. As a result, they have excess weight that carries no substance. However, you must learn to lay aside every weight that so easily besets you. You must lay aside the "base metal" that you refuse to turn into opportunity. What kind of weight do you have to lay aside?

If you are overly concerned and weighted down by the cares of life and by materiality, you have too much base metal within you. Remember, all things originate in Spirit. There is nothing that exists on the planet that has not come from that invisible realm of Spirit. If it comes from the Spirit, that is the approval that it is so in the earth.

> *There is nothing that exists on the planet that has not come from that invisible realm of Spirit.*
>
> ∼

Therefore, you are supposed to turn whatever metal is in your life into gold. However, it will not turn into gold if you fail to take its vibration and raise it to the level of gold. Jesus had the fishes and loaves. Remember the little boy was sitting there with his lunch? Jesus could have said, "Get this boy from near me." But He turned the little boy into a supermarket, and said, "Young man, come here." Jesus took the two little fishes and five loaves of bread and raised the vibration. The scripture says he lifted up his eyes. Now, you may look at this and think that Jesus lifted up his eyes toward heaven. However, that is what you see with the natural eye. But let me show you the prophetic symbolism. When He lifted up his eyes, He was lifting the vibration of the fishes and loaves. Vibration is light, and the eye deals with just light energy.

When you lift up the vibration of something you transform it. That is why Moses took a serpent that was crawling on the ground, lifted it up, and it became a healing agent. That which is considered death in its low vibration becomes life if you lift it up. If you take a creature that is poison and lift it up, the poison becomes the antidote (the cure) to the very death that is in place.

There is something in you that should be lifted up, but you are carrying around too much base metal. Many people do not know how rich they are because they are too lazy to operate as the prophetic alchemist and raise the vibration. If you get into the mystical chemist that you are, you will see some things that will turn upward for you. But you have to lay aside the base metal that you refuse to turn to opportunity. There is opportunity all around you, but you must raise it up!

~

PRINCIPLE #56

The prophetic alchemist is the prophet who knows how to go into his prophetic laboratory within and create.

~

Let me reveal one major weight that many people carry. Brace yourself because it may be a little painful when this weight is revealed. Education is a base metal that everyone carries. Some people will allow the base metal of education to sit in them in the form of a degree, a diploma from a school, or a certificate from a class. They will hang the diploma or certificate on their wall as a trophy of this major accomplishment. Some may have even graduated as valedictorian. However, if you fail to take that base metal (the degree) into your prophetic laboratory, lift the vibration of it, spin it, and turn the lead metal into gold, then you will find yourself walking around with a lot of weight but no substance.

In the same way, unless you know how to turn the truths that you receive from this book into gold, you will be weighed down with truths that will have you lead-based. Why? You have not learned how to become the prophetic alchemist and change the vibration of the "lead" that is within you into gold that will cause people to knock on your door to purchase it.

How many ideas has God given you that you have let sit? How many ideas has God given you with which you have done nothing? Let me tell you something about the prophetic alchemist, the prophetic truth-seeker. In order for any alchemy to take place, you have to do something. An unproductive prophet is a hearer of the word only. None of the truths that you read in this book are going to manifest in your life until you take the corresponding action and do something with it.

> *"Behold, I shew you a mystery; We shall not all sleep, but we shall all be changed, in a moment, in the twinkling of an eye, at the last trump: for the trumpet shall sound..."* (1 Corinthians 15:51-52)

~

PRINCIPLE #57

Seers, lift your eyes!

~

The prophet can change a situation in a moment, in the twinkling of the eye. A prophet is a seer. Therefore, if you want to change something, all you have to do is see it differently. Seers, lift your eyes! You are only as broke as you see yourself. You are only as rich as you see yourself in riches.

The prophetic alchemist has to lift the vibration by lifting up his eyes. Notice, the bread did not multiply until Jesus lifted up his eyes (not when he lifted up the bread). The boy's mother lifted up the bread earlier that day. If the vibration could have changed by lifting up the bread, it would have multiplied when the little boy lifted up the bread and gave it to Jesus. But it took the eyes of the Master to raise the vibration, and the bread multiplied.

When you start to operate as the prophetic alchemist, you will begin to change the vibration. Remember, you are the prophetic shift-shaper. You are shift-shaping. You are changing and shifting things with your eyes.

The Bible says in 1 Corinthians 15:51, *"Behold, I show you a mystery. We shall not all sleep..."* Whatever you are not experiencing, you are just asleep in it. Right now, you have <u>ALL</u> things. Everything you need is in you, but it is asleep. That is why it is a need, because it is asleep waiting for you to shake it with a vibration and move it from its slumber into an awakened state of consciousness.

You will not hear these truths taught in the average church on Sunday morning. This is why God will speak them first through the prophets. Amos 3:7 says, *"Surely the Lord thy God will do nothing, but he revealth his secret unto his servants, the prophets."* Surely, the Lord God will do "no-thing."

God reveals his secret unto his servants, the prophets. God does nothing until He converses with His servants, and the servants speak the secrets, the mysteries of God. Right now, we are fellowshipping around a mystery. The prophet's message may not be popular the first day he utters it because it is a secret. The information contained in this book can only be given to this degree because the Spirit said, "Let the secret out. Let the people know who they are. Let them know what they are ordained to come into." God could not move the planet into the next realm until He had prophets uttering the secret.

> *Everyone has the ability to be changed in a moment, in the twinkling of an eye.*
>
> ∾

Everyone is not going to stay asleep. Everyone is not going to stay poor. Somebody is going to change. Everyone has the ability to be changed in a moment, in the twinkling of an eye. The "twinkling of an eye" is not referring to your physical eyes twinkling. It is referring to your third eye, or the eyes of your understanding. The change takes place in a moment.

"We shall be changed in a moment, in the twinkling of an eye, at the last trump: for the trumpet shall sound, and the dead shall be raised incorruptible, and we shall be changed. For this corruptible must put on incorruption, and this mortal must put on immortality. So when this corruptible shall have put on incorruption, and this mortal shall have put on immortality, then shall be brought to pass the saying

that is written, Death is swallowed up in victory."
(1 Corinthians 15:52-54)

The "last trump" represents the last message that you heard, the last thought, the last truth, the last thing the Spirit uttered in your mind. When you receive the "last" revelation it does not mean the final revelation. We all are changed according to the level of the last revelation that we received.

~

PRINCIPLE #58

If it is contrary, it is only temporary.

~

There is something in you that is dead (dead to your understanding, dead to your intellect, dead to your experience), waiting for you to give it a voice and trumpet it. You are here on the planet to swallow up death. There may have been a time when sickness was plaguing your body, but you had to swallow it up in victory because it was working death in your members. There may be a day when poverty tries to creep into your life, but you have to swallow it up in victory! Whatever is contrary to what God has ordained for you, you have to learn how to swallow it up in victory!

The Bible says to call those things which be not as though they were. (Romans 4:17) In death there is life. Therefore, you have to swallow up that thing which is dead so that it may live. Moses went to God complaining, but God told him about the dense metal in his hand. Moses had to use his staff and change the vibration of it. When he was in the court of the magicians he threw his rod down and his serpent swallowed up the other serpents. The serpent swallowed it up in victory.

114

You have to know how to swallow up what is contrary, because if it is contrary, it is only temporary.

You may be in a situation right now that is contrary, but I want to give you the Word of the Lord and let you know that it is only temporary! If you don't like what is going on, I dare you to wink! The next time you see an adversary say, "Listen, don't let me wink at you. I am going to change this situation in a moment, in the twinkling of an eye!"

Scatter!

"A king that sitteth on the throne of judgment scattereth away all evil with his eyes." (Proverbs 20:8)

We shift the things with our eyes or with our mind. The words "eyes" and "mind" are synonymous. How do you scatter the evil away with your eyes? When you see only God you crowd out of visibility anything that is other than God. You scatter the evil with your eyes. As the prophet, you have to be able to sit as a king in judgment and master the art of scattering evil with your eyes. When you operate in the mind of the Spirit you will learn how to move forward with the Seeing Eye.

Proverbs 20:12 says, *"The hearing ear, and the Seeing Eye, the LORD hath made even both of them."* The ear and the eye are prophetic instruments. The prophet hears the word of the Lord, and the prophet sees the vision of the Lord. Are your ears anointed to hear - Are you hearing? Are your eyes anointed to see - Are you seeing? Are you using both tools that the Lord has made? Think about it, the Lord would not have made the eyes and the ears if they could not bring glory to His name.

~

PRINCIPLE #59

When you see ONLY God, you crowd all
negativity out of the picture.

~

Proverbs 20:8, in the New Living Translation says, *"When a king judges he carefully weighs all of the evidence."* The prophet is supposed to weigh it in the mind of the Spirit and distinguish the bad from the good. How do you distinguish bad from good? By what you choose to see. Hold fast to that which is good and see the bad out of existence. How do you see the bad out of existence? By not putting any value on it and crowding it out, seeing only good, seeing only God. When you see only God, you crowd all negativity out of the picture. This is how you scatter evil with your eyes.

The Amplified Versions says, *"A king who sits on the throne of judgment winnows out all evil like shaft with his eyes..."* The eyes are the windows of the soul. The prophet operates from a sacred place, which is a laboratory. As the seer, the prophet filters out evil with his eyes. Hearing takes place on many different levels. If you look at hearing, the ear is connected with the eyes (pupils). Are your pupils hearing? Notice, your pupils and your ears look like seeds. If you look at your ear it looks like an embryo. You have to watch who is in your ear, because whoever is in your ear is growing something in your mind.

It is very important that we take note of what it is that we are hearing because that is a seed growing in us. We have to watch what we are seeing because that is seed growing in us. The only thing in your experience is what you see.

> "A king that sitteth in the throne of judgment scattereth away all evil with his eyes. Who can say, I have made my heart clean, I am pure from my sin? Divers weights, and divers measures, both of them are alike abomination to the Lord. Even a child is known by his doings, whether his work be pure or whether it be right. The hearing ear, and the seeing eye, the Lord hath made even both of them. Love not sleep..." (Proverbs 20:8-13 (KJV)

The scripture says, "Love not sleep, lest thou come to poverty..." Poverty only happens to the unaware. Poverty only takes place to those who are asleep. Poverty is only happening to those who refuse to winnow it out. Poverty is the result of sleep. Why would God tell you not to love sleep? If you are sleep, your eyes are not scattering away evil. If you are asleep, nothing can grow around you. Because a person's eyes are open physically doesn't mean they are awake. We all sleep collectively and awaken individually.

The scripture goes on to say, "...open thine eyes and thou shalt be satisfied with bread."

How am I going to be satisfied with bread? I am going to use my seeing eye. Seers are supposed to be prosperous, if they are true seers. If they are not prosperous, then they are false seers. So, if you are not prosperous, the answer is simple; your eyes are shut and you are sleeping.

⌒

PRINCIPLE #60

We all sleep collectively and awaken individually.

⌒

You can only know that which you are. You are your own self-knowledge. You are the self-knowledge of yourself. You are only as large as YOU. You can only come to be YOU. Remember, *"God stands in the assembly of the representatives of gods."* God only stands in His many disguises that are re-presenting Him. So, who am I? I am God. Define the **YOU** of you? I am re-presenting God though I am in the form of Bernard. When you represent, you are "re-presenting" Him. You bring the presence back again. So, every one of us are here on the planet "re-presenting" God, "presenting" Him again. The question is, is God present in you?

The Way Of The Prophet

I am ready to take those who are seers into the next dimension of their seership. I am ready to take those who are true seers and true prophets into their visionary ability, so that they can become individuals who have the ability to turn thoughts into things, to take the invisible and make it visible, and to understand the process. Therefore, it is important to understand some things about the ways of the prophet.

There is a process that you have to go through in order to manifest God in your life and to be God. God always teaches us the unknown by the known. That is spiritual law. God teaches us about the things which are unseen by the things which are seen. God takes that which is tangible and uses it. Jesus spoke in parables. He used an earthly setting to explain spiritual truths. By reading this book, I want to bring you into higher spiritual truths. I want to get you to the point where you are "caught up to meet him in the air," caught up to meet Him in thought, in consciousness. When you are caught up in consciousness, it is difficult to be grounded by fundamentals. What you see is not your base reality. You have to "grow up into Him."

~

PRINCIPLE #61

God is calling you to __KNOW__ who you are.

~

Paul said, *"Let this mind be in you which is also in Christ Jesus. Who, being in the form of God, thought it not robbery to be equal with God: But made himself of no reputation, and took upon him the form of a servant..."* (Philippians 2:5-7) You are in the form of God. However, the difference between you and Jesus is that He thought it was not robbery to be equal with God, but you think it is robbery. As long as you think it is robbery to be equal with God you are being robbed of God.

Jesus was a prophetic shape-shifter. You are supposed to know that you are God, and then make yourself into whatever earthly likeness you desire to be. When you get tired of being poor, shape-shift and begin to be God playing rich.

"And he said unto me, It is done. I am Alpha and Omega, the beginning and the end. I will give unto

him that is athirst of the fountain of the water of life freely. He that overcometh shall inherit all things; and I will be his God, and he shall be my son. But the fearful, and unbelieving, and the abominable, and the murders, and the whoremongers, and the sorcerers, and idolaters, and all liars, shall have their part in the lake which burneth with fire and brimstone: which is the second death. " (Revelation 21:6-8)

Jesus said it is done. He will give to those who thirst, the fountain from the water of life freely. God will allow you to go through hell so you can thirst, and then—He gives you the fountain from the water of life freely. God will put you in the lake of fire so you can thirst—He wants to give you the water of life freely. Don't be afraid of hell. Just get thirsty there so that—He can give you the water of life freely. There must be a thirst!

Verse 7 in the Amplified bible says, *"He who is victorious shall inherit all things, and I shall be God to him, and he shall be My son."* God wants you to be victorious. He wants you to be an overcomer. If you are not an overcomer and you are not victorious, then you are not really moving in the fullness of sonship. So he has to throw you in hell so you can thirst. Otherwise you will not be a Son.

God does not want you to have to work for it. He just wants you to thirst for it. *"He that hunger and thirst after righteousness shall be filled."* (Matthew 5:6) You cannot be filled if there is no hunger and thirst. Think about it - When the children of Israel came out of Egypt, why did they get punished? Why weren't they able to go into Canaan Land? A journey that should have taken maybe 40 days or so to complete, took them 40 years? Why did it take them 40 years? They weren't hungry enough. God will keep you in hell until you get thirsty enough.

Some people are happy with certain clothing, happy where they are living, and God says, "Okay, that will be you." But when you become thirsty for something better, that is when God gives you better. You have to drink your way out of your experience!

~

PRINCIPLE #62

God will keep you in hell until you
get thirsty enough.

~

The children of Israel kept feeding from the same memory. When faced with a challenge they always remembered what they received back in Egypt. They never fully divorced the other self, the other life. It was like they were living in adultery. They kept going back to the old mind and never embraced the new mind into which they were brought.

> *But the fearful, and unbelieving, and the abominable, and the murders, and the whoremongers, and the sorcerers, and idolaters, and all liars, shall have their part in the lake which burneth with fire and brimstone: which is the second death."* (Revelation 21:8)

The fearful are the individuals who are cowards, those who are fearful to be God. "I don't know if I can say, 'I am God.' I don't play with God like that. You won't catch me saying I am God. There is only one God, and He says, 'I am God and beside me there is no other.'" Now, that is true, but why would you be beside Him as another? You are focusing on becoming separate and apart from God in your personality, when you need to become one with Him in principle, understanding that you, in personality, are nothing because all there is, is God.

The murderers are those who will murder God in them. They understand that they are born of God, but they keep killing Him by saying, "I'm not Him." Monkeys beget monkeys, cats beget cats, and cows beget cows. Therefore, God begets gods. Figure it out. How can you be something other than who God is? Every time you hear "Ye are Gods," you see a physical face. However, no one can see God and live. God is principle. God is Spirit incarnating Himself in a person, to demonstrate a truth unto humanity.

The whoremongers are those who are sleeping with a god other than the one God who says, "I am God." The Bible says that you should not go whoring after other gods. The sorcerers and idolaters are those individuals who try to access power outside of God. Some people believe that the Bible speaks against star-gazing, which is true. It speaks about those who were trying to do it outside of God. If you believe that was wrong, then you have to cancel out the wise men, because they were all astrologers.

Joseph understood astrology. He looked up into the heavens and saw the moon, the sun, and the eleven stars. He knew that the sun was his father, the moon was his mother, and the eleven stars were his brethren. He understood that they were all walking planets. In the same way, the prophets must understand the science of the heavens and the science of the earth. The science of the heavens is the science of the stars, and the science of the earth is the science of numbers. Unless you understand numerology and astrology, you are going to miss the whole message of the seven stars, which is always speaking to the seven churches, which is always talking to your seven energy systems, which is speaking to all seven of your bodies.

Some people believe that the Bible speaks against those who talk to the dead. Of course it does, if it is outside of Christ. That is considered sorcery. But explain Jesus in the Mount of Transfiguration with two dead people. Then we see in the scriptures where the prophet lays on the body of a dead child. How do you think he brought his spirit back? Do you think he brought his spirit back by dealing with his physical dense body? Evidently, the prophet had to use another body, possibly his ghost body, to go grab the hand of the child's ghost and say, "Don't leave home yet. Come on back. Your work is not complete."

There are so many dimensions for God to dwell, but we limit God to this one physical body.

There are so many dimensions for God to dwell, but we limit God to this one physical body. So when people hear somebody saying, "I am God," many see a 5' 7" man saying, "I am God." However, you are looking at a personality in a dense body, which is just a carrier of God (or maybe I should say God is carrying the physical body). How can your physical body contain God? God really contains you. It only looks like you are containing Him. God contains you and then personifies Himself through you.

～

PRINCIPLE #63

Do not limit god to the physical body.

～

Acts 17:28 says, *"In Him we live, and move and have our being."* We have our being in God. Moving and having is all happening, and it is happening in Him. One songwriter said, "Just one look." If you just look at it differently, it will shift.

"Trance-Former"

"I beseech you, therefore, brethren, by the mercies of God, that ye present your bodies a living sacrifice, holy, acceptable unto God, which is your reasonable service. And be not conformed to this world: but be ye transformed by the renewing of your mind." (Romans 12:1-2)

"This book of the law shall not depart out of thy mouth; but thou shalt meditate therein day and night, that thou mayest observe to do according to all that is written therein: for then thou shalt make thy way prosperous, and then thou shalt have good success." (Joshua 1:8)

Meditation is vital in changing your thoughts into things. Meditation is a mental exercise in which you sit still and allow your mind to concentrate (or go into a trance). You are the "host" and meditation is the "guest." You will only see things transform when you can go into a trance and start forming them another way in your mind. You must change your thoughts. Oftentimes, your meditation is your medication. You have to be "tranced" in order to form. In martial arts, meditation is used as a form of concentration. In order for a martial artist to break a block of wood, he/she is taught to see past, or see beyond, the wood that they see. They are taught that if they see the wood they will stop. Their hand will remind them that they only saw to the level of the wood. However, meditation brings you to a level of consciousness where you begin to see beyond the wood, beyond physical realm.

Phil. 4:8 says, *Finally, brethren, whatsoever things are true, whatsoever things are honest, whatsoever things are just, whatsoever things are pure, whatsoever things are lovely, whatsoever things are of good report; if there be any virtue, and if there be any praise, think on these things."* When you think on (meditate) the right thoughts, you will change your thoughts into things. You have to see beyond your present condition. Meditation is a process of evolution where you transform not only yourself, but also your surroundings in life. When you enter into meditation you have to drop the mind. The mind will always try to trick you out of your birthright and try to get you to second-guess or doubt yourself.

It is like the story of Jacob and Esau. You have to send the mind out into the field hunting - "Go do something. Go occupy yourself." The eldest son had the birthright that the younger son wanted to have. The father sent the eldest son out into the field to get him something to eat, while the younger son stayed home with mother.

~

PRINCIPLE #64

*You have the ability to change your
thoughts into things.*

~

Give your mind something else to do, and while it is away, begin to become the very son that the father hears. While the eldest son is out concerned with things (while you are out chasing the effects), the younger son (the subconscious mind), is at home being dressed up for the part. Father (conscious mind) is blind to what the subconscious is transforming, because your subconscious mind is ten times stronger than your conscious mind. Your subconscious mind will always return to you what you say you are, or even what you say you are not.

So, while the mind is away (while you are in meditation), mother is dressing you up. Mother is feeling nature. You must get into the state of what it feels like to be that and then you "occupy that state until it comes." Until the physical effects of that state begin to manifest, you have to occupy the feeling of it. You have to hover there, stay there, and live in that state. Don't create the state, just live there, and when it comes, it will come quickly, and you will be the very thing upon which you meditated.

You have to recognize and understand the truth of you. See beyond your present condition. See past your present state. You have to go into your lab, into your physical body. When was the last time you went to work in your lab? Your physical body is just a laboratory for you to do your mystical work, to do the work of the prophet, to handle the mysteries, and to turn thoughts into things. You have to see beyond your present condition!

∼

PRINCIPLE #65

Lay aside any "base metal" you refuse to turn into opportunity.

∼

CHAPTER 8

THE INVISIBLE PROPHET

+—·—·—

Prophetic Consciousness

"And God said, Let us make man in our image, after our likeness: and let them have dominion over the fish of the sea, and over the fowl of the air, and over the cattle, and over all the earth, and over every creeping thing that creepeth upon the earth. So God created man in his own image, in the image of God created he him; male and female created he them. And God blessed them, and God said unto them, Be fruitful..." (Genesis 1:26-28)

The image and likeness of God speaks of His visible representation, the exact likeness, having a striking appearance of God in manner and thought. We are in the image of God. We are heirs and joint heirs with Jesus Christ. Thus, the prophet is to be found in the brightness of His glory as the perfect imprint and representation of His Person. God has delegated His grace and authority unto His prophets, an innate ability to maintain, to guide and to propel the people of God by the prophetic word. God is the foundation of all prophets, being made in the similitude of God's identity.

Image is very important. The image you portray is the outgrowth of the knowledge that you have accumulated and it streamlines your thought process. The image you portray determines the thoughts that reside in your mind. Exodus 20:4 says, *"Thou shalt not make unto thee any graven image, or any likeness of anything that is in the heaven above, or that is in the earth beneath, or that is in the water under the earth."* God was against graven images because He already made you in His image and in His likeness.

Therefore, the prophet must know God in order to come into the consciousness of God. Prophetic consciousness is God consciousness. If you become conscious of God, you will walk in the prophetic understanding of what God is doing. You will be a refresher to someone who is dwelling on dry land; you will become the water for which they thirst.

~

PRINCIPLE #66

You are made in the image and likeness of god.

~

The Void

"In the beginning God created the heaven and the earth…" (Genesis 1:1) Anything you create must first be created with heaven in view. Many people are working for

earthly things and have forsaken heavenly things. However, in order to become a co-creator with God, you must go back to the beginning to see how God created. Your first creation should be heaven, a state of mind that is heavenly, a state of mind that is Godly, a state of mind that is not looking for earthly manifestation. After you create a heavenly mindset, then comes the earthly manifestation. *"Thy will be done in earth as it is in heaven..."* (Matt. 6:10)

Heaven is the cause. Some people chase the effects and separate themselves from the cause. However, don't get so lost in the drama of the effects of your creation that you forget heaven and become bound to earth. If you don't have a heavenly mindset, the earthly manifestation may seem impossible, because anything God creates is without form and it is void.

Nature abhors a void. The visions and dreams that God gives to you to bring to fruition are always without form and void in the beginning. God has to put you in a void in order for you to know how it feels, so that when the miracles happen and your dreams and visions are manifested you can testify to the greatness of God. This is fullness. Then when you get to the fullness, He has to take you to the next level, which is, again, the void.

For example, you rent your first apartment. It is a one-room apartment. You are so glad to have the one room. Then God gives you the means to fill the one room. Now, you are really excited. *"Wow, I have a new bed, new dresser."* Suddenly, the one bedroom is too small. There is not enough space. Then God says to go and get a three-bedroom apartment. You find the three bedroom apartment and move immediately. You just left fullness (the one room apartment) and went back to the void (the three-bedroom apartment).

Then God gives you the means to fill the three-bedroom apartment. The three-bedroom apartment is comfortable for a while, but then it starts to feel too small. So God says, "Now, I want you to go and get the house." You purchase the new house. Now, you are in the void again. Not only are you in the void, but you are struggling at every level. The struggle is not because the devil is attacking your finances; you are in a void. Now you are in a position to create again. You must find God in the void. When you are thankful in the void, God fills the void.

For many people, once they get to fullness they remember what it was like to be in the void and they say, "Never again." However, if you say "never again" to the void, you curse yourself and end up in a rut, because God's footsteps are in the deep, and he operates in the void. Jesus told His disciples to launch out into the deep, a place where it seemed like they would not catch any fish, but that was the very place that God manifested what they needed. God is always in a spot that is deeper than you are willing to walk.

$\sim$

PRINCIPLE #67

God is always in a spot that is deeper than
you are willing to walk.

$\sim$

You cannot achieve success without hard work. Success never comes before work. Many people miss opportunities because they are blinded by the hard work. Some people miss opportunities because their main focus is money. They are so driven by how much money they will make that they miss the joy of watching the void filled. However, if you are working for the pay, you are a mercenary.

"...and darkness was on the face of the deep. And the Spirit of God moved upon the face of the waters. And God said, 'Let there be light,' and there was light. And God saw the light that it was good; and God divided the light from the darkness." (Genesis 1:2-4)

God said, "let there be," and then God saw. Not only did God have to speak his dream into manifestation, but He then had to visualize it. Once you have spoken your dream into existence, and called it forth out of the heavenly realm, you must then visualize it. If you do not see it after you say it, you will not get it. You have to see it in your imagination.

> *Once you have spoken your dream into existence, and called it forth out of the heavenly realm, you must then visualize it.*
> ⌇

The Amplified Bible says, *"In the beginning God created, (prepared, formed, fashioned) the heavens and earth..."* Your dream has to be prepared, formed and fashioned in your mind before you enjoy fruit of it. How prepared is your dream in you? Are you dubious in your consciousness, wavering back and forth between two thoughts, two twins within you debating whether it is good or bad? You must make a decision. In your own mindset you have to reconcile. The word "reconciliation" means, to make friendly again. You have to take the two opposing thoughts and make them friendly, make them fall in love with each other once again so that your dream can come to full manifestation.

Many people have become hostile to their Creator and therefore, hostile to themselves. Reconciliation is about making God your friend again. Many people have lost their friendship with Him and their love for Him, because they do not like His ways. However, if you love His ways, you will do His acts and carry out His plan for your life. You will follow the contract. If you really love Him, your work will demonstrate that you love Him, and that you are Him.

~

PRINCIPLE #68

Your dream has to be prepared, formed and fashioned in your mind before you enjoy fruit of it.

~

The Waste Place

"And the earth was without form and an empty waste. And darkness was upon the face of the very great deep..." (Genesis 1:2, Amplified Version)

We can see from the scripture that the earth had problems. It was without form and described as an "empty waste." Oftentimes, God will throw you into problem situations, and in places that appear empty (waste places) so that you can work it out. God will put you in a waste place so that you can make it a God space. However, when you do not honor the waste places of life, you will fail to get your proper space in life.

"The Spirit of God was moving (hovering, brooding) over the face of the waters. And God said, 'Let there be light,' and there was light. And God saw that the light was good (suitable, pleasant) and he approved it..." (Genesis 1:2-4, Amplified Version)

Notice what God did when He saw the light; He approved it. How many situations has God put you in that were waste places, but you never approved them? You never said, "I can work with this." You couldn't project the light into it, so you kept seeing it as a waste place, an indecent place, instead of the "fullness of God" place. However, you have to be careful when you ask God to bless you, because He may throw you into a waste place. He will throw you into a season where you will be in the void. He will put you in a vacuum. In other words, He will vacuum clean what you were in before, and then throw you into a new void so that you can have the joy of discovering, once again, that you are a co-creator with God.

Now, what are you waiting for to get your next piece of real estate? Are you afraid of the void? Are you afraid of the waste place? Are you worried that you will not be able to afford it? You may not be able to afford it. But God is all in all. He has the situation under control, and He provides in the void. He is the beginning, the cause and the source of all that is. Unless you see God with prophetic eyes, you will be limited in experience.

You have to prophesy in the void. You have to use faith to call forth those things which be not as though they were. You must prophesy in the void, prophesy in the darkness; prophesy in the unseen; prophesy when you can't see it; prophesy when you can't feel it; prophesy when you can't hear it; prophesy when it is not in sight; prophesy when it is out of reach; prophesy in the cursed place; prophesy in the confused place; prophesy in the place of sickness; prophesy in the place of disease; prophesy in the midst of a person's poverty; prophesy in the bankruptcy; prophesy in the cursed place. That is the Power of Prophecy!

~

PRINCIPLE #69

God works in the void.

~

CHAPTER 9

PICTURE THIS!

—·—·≡◆≡·—·—

"The imagination may be compared to Adam's dream—he awoke and found it truth." The whole creation is essentially subjective, and the dream is the theater where the dreamer is at once scene, actor, prompter, stage manager, author, audience and critic."
—Psychological Reflections: A Jung Anthology

Divine Imagination

"Thus the heavens and the earth were finished, and all the host of them." (Genesis 2:1)

God created everything in His imagination, and on the seventh day he rested His mind. God's creation project was finished in God's mind. It was finished in His imagination.

When you are a dreamer, you have to take risks. The Bible says, *"...and God separated the light from the darkness."* (Genesis 1:4) The imagination may be compared to

Adam's dream. God put Adam in a deep sleep. When Adam awakened he found Eve. He found himself. Eve came out of Adam. You may find yourself in a deep sleep. However, the Lord is getting ready to awaken you. Now, don't scream at what you find, because you are going to only find yourself.

It is important for you to know yourself and to be able to correct yourself. Right now, you are awakening to truth, and you may not like what you see. However, no one can come into your life unless it's you, for you only meet yourself. Your dream is what you want to become, to do, or to have during your lifetime. What do you want to do? What do you want to become? What do you want to have during your lifetime? That is your dream. Your dream will become you the moment you choose for your dream to become reality.

Your dream will become you the moment you choose for your dream to become reality

~

However, you have to approve of it. Until you give yourself permission within to have the dream, the dream will never happen for you.

Whatever you don't have today, it is because you haven't given yourself the permission to have it. You haven't given yourself the permission to be it. You haven't given yourself the permission to enjoy it. Give yourself permission. What are you waiting for?

Even God saw it and approved it. God is waiting for you to grade what is in your imagination (your heavenly state of mind), before He manifests your dreams in the earth realm.

~

PRINCIPLE #70

*Your dream will become you the moment you
choose for your dream to become reality.*

~

The moment you begin to move toward your dream,
your relationships will change. Once you accept and
embrace your dream everyone in your dream will start to
gravitate towards you. Many people don't embrace their
dreams because they already know that certain people are
not in their dreams. It is imperative that you understand who
is in your future. Allow your dream to be alive in you and not
stolen from you. Your dream will be alive the moment you
start to celebrate the person you are called to be, and you
will discover the truth of you in every move that you make.
You meet only the individuals within your environment that
you have entertained in your mind. You can only meet people who are in your environment. Believe it or not, you create the surroundings.

Your dream will always demand from you uncommon
faith. You must have uncommon faith in order for your dream
to be realized, the kind of faith that will bring your dream from
"make-believe" to "made-to-be-believed." You have to make
some moves. What moves do you have to make?

Your dream starts as a fantasy, but you can't let it remain
a fantasy. Move the fantasy to a place of reality. If you constantly see your dream as a fantasy, you will never experience the reality of it. Fantasy comes from the Greek word,
phantasia, meaning appearance, image, perception. What

are you telegraphing? What kind of thoughts are you sending? Fantasy is the use of the imagination. It starts in the mind. Children fantasize. The scripture says, *"Except you become as a little child, you shall not enter into the kingdom of heaven)."* (Matthew 18:3) You have to take your dream and grow it up from the child state into the adult state.

Your dream will expose every adversary of the dream once it appears that the dream can be a reality. Once you embrace the dream, it will expose every enemy. Therefore, you must practice continual visualization of your dream, and then allow your dream to go from visualization to materialization. The passion for your dream must be so strong that it burns within you without the encouragement of others.

~

PRINCIPLE #71

Your dream will demand uncommon faith.

~

Inner Eye or Outer Eye

Need exists when you see things from the material plane. Whenever you have a need in life it is because you are trapped in the material plane. You are trapped in man's kingdom, instead of God's kingdom.

Many people have created the idea of need out of their experience, the idea that they need things in order to survive. That need is created out of their imagination. Still others think they need a degree to earn a certain income. However, they are working outside of principle. They are reaching for something outside of them instead of for the One who is inside of them. Henry Ford only had an eighth grade education, but he developed one of the most success-ful companies in the world. I am not against education, but don't substitute your education for the kingdom. Never let anything outside of the kingdom demand more of your mind than the kingdom itself.

> *"The light of the body is the eye: therefore, when thine eye is single, thy whole body also is full of light; but when thine eye is evil, thy body also is full of darkness."* (Luke 11:34)

Truth is to be found in the back of the eye. The light of the body is the eye. Are you living according to what you see with the inner eye or the outer eye? The outer eye is looking at the realm of materiality, things, circumstances, and hard facts. The inner eye is looking at the riches that are within. *"I can do all things through Christ, which strength-eneth me."* (Philippians 4:13) You should not look outside of you for the blessings of God because the blessings are on the inside of you. Stop looking to a God out there. Who is out there? Jesus came teaching you that the kingdom of God is within. Therefore, you should not look outside of you.

Can you imagine what would happen if the entire com-munity became single-eyed, if we all saw one thing? That is power. When the people become one there is power. It is impossible for you not to survive. Our enemies are those who refuse to be one with us. You cannot fail to live. It is not a question of whether you will live, but how. What form will you take? You have to live some kind of life, but what kind of form will it be? Will it be deformed?

What you see with your outer eye is an illusion (ill-usion). It is "ill." All things seek containment. Everything seeks to be contained somewhere. Spirit looks to be housed. Spirit seeks for a body in which to live. When your eye becomes single, the rest of the body gets full of light. You're seeing determines your being. You will be changed in a moment, in the twinkling of an eye, if you just see things differently with your inner eye. The twinkling of the eye determines what you will be changed into at that moment.

~

PRINCIPLE #72

What you see with your outer eye is only an illusion.

~

The outer eye operates in illusion. The outer eye is always doing things based on facts. For example, when you purchase a home, the bank will ask you for the facts. *"How much money do you have? Where is your check? Can you bring in your pay stubs?"* However, you have to know how to overcome those obstacles. Don't let anyone corner you with a lot of facts. You must say in your subconscious, "Get me someone that understands Spirit."

The eyes see what the mind believes. John 1:3, *"All things were made,"* by him; and without him was not any-thing made that was made."* All things were made by him. Therefore, all things are made by you. The scripture says to *"Seek ye first the kingdom of God, and all of these things shall be added."* Things will be added to you because you seek after the kingdom. You produce the cause by seeking. *"Seek and ye shall find."* (Matthew 7:7)

If you seek the kingdom, you will find things. You may feel that you lack certain things in your life that you desire. However, you have just revealed to yourself that you haven't been seeking the kingdom. Why don't you get into prayer? But before you get into prayer, make sure you seek the kingdom. Don't seek God, because you can seek God and miss the kingdom. The Bible says that you should meditate day and night. Meditate on the kingdom and God will produce the things.

Visualization is the key to prayer.

Many people pray with their problem in mind. However, this magnifies the image. Change the image in your imagination, and then maintain the desired result.

You have to see your desire only. There are too many other images floating in your mind. Get rid of the illusions and see Jesus only (the desire), and then just like God, you rest after your creation. You rest in the fact that it is done. It is finished.

God is all-science. Visualization is the key to prayer. According to mind science, when we pray, we should face a mental direction, not a physical direction. In visualization, you must make sure you mentally face the right direction. You want to make sure that what you desire is coming in the right entrance. Many people pray, but they pray from the state of the problem. That is why the problem repeats itself.

When Jesus said He lifted up his eyes he did not lift his physical eyes. Many people have lifted up their physical eyes and came back to the same problem. Therefore, it must be something more than lifting up of a physical eye, or doing something in the physical body. There are eyes behind the eyes. There is a world that is more real behind your eyes than the world that is before your eyes.

You cannot hold fast to what you see with your physical eyes because it doesn't speak the truth. The truth is behind the eyes. When Jesus was getting ready to be taken off the scene, he informed His disciples that as long as the bridegroom is present they don't need to fast. But when He is taken away, then you are going to have to fast. You are going to have to fast from the external facts, and then you have to only see the Christ that is within you rising up and then projecting the desired result, not the external facts. The external facts will lie to you. The only truth is the truth that comes from within you. Truth is birthed from within, never from without. When you understand that truth is birthed from within, then you will start creating that situation from the inside. When you create it from the inside, there will be no lack in your life.

God has already given you everything you need to create the promise He has made to you and bring it into manifestation. Whatever promise God has made to you, He has already created it for you through something that already exists in your life. If God tells you He is going to make you great and bring you before nations, then there is something that is in your hand and in your house that is going to bring you there. However, you must discern what it is. If God told you that He is going to make you wealthy, then there is something in your hand and in your house that is going to make you wealthy. It's not something that you are going to have to go outside to bring in, but it's something that is already within your reach.

144

Technique of Prayer

Face the south wall in your home, or directional south. Let the macrocosm be the house, and your mental state be the microcosm. If you face the south, the east is going to be on your left and the west is going to be on your right. Whatever image you want to bring to pass, you must put it to the east of your temple. Put it at the left of your mental state, and then visualize what you want. The sun rises first in the east and then it sets in the west. So you put the photograph in the east, visualize it in the east, and hold it in your imagination until you can feel it in your present. That is how you bring it to pass. Anything that has already been brought to pass and you want to redo the experience, just grab it from the west and ask for it to repeat itself.

The Contemplative Life

Prayer is inner communion. No longer pray for the things of this world, because without the realization of the presence and power of God within you, you will not receive the things of God. The nature of prayer should change, no longer begging, but true getting, contemplating the presence of God within.

> *"And Jesus answering saith unto them, Have faith in God. For verily I say unto you, whosoever shall say unto this mountain, "Be thou removed, and be thou cast into the sea and shall not doubt in his heart but shall believe that those things which he saith shall come to pass; he shall have whatsoever he saith." (Mark 11:22-24)*

When the scripture says, "have faith in God," it means have the God-kind of faith, or have the same faith that God has. Learn how to "say" before "doing." God said, "Let there be light," and there was light. He never "did" light. He just said, "Let be," and then He became still.

The Scripture says, *"...whosoever shall say unto this mountain, 'Be thou removed and be thou cast into the sea' and shall not doubt in his heart..."* (Mark 11:23) In other words, do not allow your heart to get into duality. Do not have two minds you should only have one mind. You have to believe your own journalism about yourself. Until you believe in yourself, others cannot believe in you.

"...Therefore I say unto you, what things soever ye desire, when ye pray, believe that you receive them, and ye shall have them." (Mark 11:25) You don't have to chase things. All you have to do is just believe that you received them. If you have a bountiful eye, if you see much for yourself, you will be blessed. How bountiful is your eye? It will determine how blessed you are. If you can't see it, you will never be it. So, whatever things you desire when you pray, believe that you receive them, and you shall have them.

~

PRINCIPLE #73

Whatever things you desire when you pray, believe that you receive them, and you shall have them.

~

Never pray for something outside of you. Seek only for the inner communion with the "I Am" Presence of God within you. For example, if you pray for a house, you are in sin, because you just separated yourself from the house. This is why Jesus said, "what things soever ye desire when ye pray." Jesus was saying, "Hold it, don't come to me about things in prayer. Just believe that you receive them and you shall have them."

You should not be in a place where you are struggling for full baskets. Just be the fullness of every basket around you. There are many things that come up and Spirit will say, *"Okay, you know what you have to do. Remember the last lesson I taught you?"* "Yes, Lord, be still." Let be and be still." Then people look up and say, *"But wait a minute, this is the situation that is at hand right now."* They will give you a hard fact. A hard fact is one that will look good on the paper.

But you have to begin to dialogue with yourself in your own consciousness. "What are you going to do?" "I am going to let be and be still." "Why?" "Because something is trying to keep me from knowing and understanding that I am God. Something is trying to get me in crisis mode. Something is trying to get me into an emergency."

Jesus said Lazarus was sleeping. However, Mary said, "Lazarus is dead. Jesus that is your friend. You should have been there when you got the first notice." Then a friend of Jesus came and brought him a hard fact. "He stinks! Roll the stone away." But Jesus said "Let be and be still! Don't get in a panic."

God wants to get you to the point where you can just let be. Just be filled! God said, Let there be light. Let there be a firmament in heaven. Let there be fish in the sea. Let there be fowl in the air. Let there be. Let be; let be; and just be still and know that I am God.

The only struggle you should have is just being still and knowing that I Am. Let go of God for the sake of God. Most people are praying to a God outside of themselves. Let go of God for the sake of God. God's exit is his entrance. The more you seek God, the less you will find God. Maybe that's why you are supposed to be seeking first the kingdom. Find the system, and stop looking at a personality. God does not ask anything else of you except that you let yourself go and let God be God in you.

~

PRINCIPLE #74

Let be and be still!

~

The reason why you may not be receiving is because you're not letting. The moment I can let be and be still, that is the moment that God can be God in me. What are you ready for God to be? Now, He is going to ask you to empty out something. The Bible says that you cannot put new wine in old wineskins. There has to be an emptying out, a losing of everything so you can have all things.

If you are struggling financially, then I would have to ask you the simple question, What little are you holding onto that God is demanding you to release? There is something you are hiding. Nature abhors a void, so does God.

There is something that God wants to get into your life, but you must begin to meditate day and night. Going into meditation is like going back into the darkness, where everything is Spirit. That is the source of where your supply is coming from before it hardens into a fact, before it materializes. But you must go into the darkness. You have to be like Jacob and begin to trick the father. You have to refuse to go out into the field, which is the facts, the outer world, but go back into the house, which is in your imagination, and you meet with mother (your subconscious mind) there, and let her dress you up. "Do you feel like you deserve what you are asking me for?" "Do you really believe that you are what you say you are?" And then you say, "Yes, I am your very son Esau." "Mother" (your subconscious mind) teaches you how to lie to the facts.

Meditation teaches you how to die. It prepares you for death. In this part of the world we are afraid of death. But meditation teaches you how to die, and once you die you go within yourself. You become like the baby. The baby doesn't breathe by itself. It lives in water. It lives in an unformed substance. The baby begins to live off of the mother. So you have to die to self, go within, and now you can begin to live off of "mother" (your subconscious mind).

Meditation teaches you how to die. It prepares you for death.

Darkness is the place of unformed purposes. Mother (subconscious) is asking you, "What do you want formed?" You have to close your eyes and go to a deeper level in mind, a deeper level of consciousness.

> *"And on the seventh day God ended his work which he had made; and he rested on the seventh day from all his work which he had made. And God blessed the seventh day, and sanctified it: because that in it he had rested from all his work which God created and made."* (Genesis 2:2-3)

149

God rested on the seventh day, which signifies that he went into meditation. He rested from all of His work in creation. God works from the beginning to the end, and then from the end to the beginning. Once something is complete in your mind, then the manifestation of those things begins to take place. All of a sudden, the order starts coming. For example, when you get the house that you purchase in your mind the house doesn't just appear. The banker appears, and the realtor appears. I don't see the house yet, but I am seeing the signs of the house. All of a sudden, a millionaire appears that says, "I want to underwrite something that you are doing for your business." But it doesn't start appearing until it has rested in your mind.

~

PRINCIPLE #75

*Your subconscious mind teaches you how
to lie to the facts.*

~

"These are the generations of the heavens and of the earth when they were created, in the day that the Lord God made the earth and the heavens. And every plant of the field before it was in the earth, and every herb of the field before it grew: for the Lord God had not caused it to rain upon the earth, and there was not a man to till the ground." (Genesis 2:4-5)

Now, we have a ground, but there is no man to till it. Man was created, but God said there is no man to till the ground; there was no manifestation of the man He just created. The truth is there was man, but no man to till. There is a difference between man created and man "form-ated." There is a difference in created in your imagination. All things are thoughts and thoughts are things. All thoughts are things, and nothing becomes a thing until you can freeze that thought into your imagination. The only thing that exists in the earth realm is just frozen thought.

So there was no man, and the Lord God formed man. (Genesis 2:7) He formed man that He had already created and imagined. So, Genesis 1 is God creating in Spirit, and Genesis 2 is God forming what was in His imagination.

Cultivation Of Concentration

Until there is the cultivation of concentration, until you can get focused, you will be miserable in life. You have to get focused in order to see success. Concentration is bringing the mind to a center and keeping it there. It is vitally necessary to the accomplishment of any task. The way you kill a man with a dream is to take him off focus by giving him another dream. Be very careful when many people are piling stuff on your plate. Every harvest that appears may not be God. You can get a harvest that becomes so overwhelming that you are unable to manage it and it becomes a curse. What good is a drought, if when the rain comes down it is too much, and you begin to drown?

It is a curse when you are not prepared for success. How prepared are you for success? How prepared are you to be an achiever?

Concentration is the father of thoroughness and the mother of excellence. I am getting out of debt. I am becoming a high achiever. I am going to be the head and not the tail. I will move with thoroughness and excellence. This is concentration. This is divine order, and it is in order. Every successful person must practice the power of concentration. The fixing of the eyes upon an object or symbol is just the beginning. The power of seeing is the ability to come into the divine law of getting. When you understand the power of seeing you will understand having, doing, and being.

~

PRINCIPLE #76

Concentration is the father of thoroughness and the mother of excellence.

~

What Do You See?

"Behold, he cometh with clouds; and every eye shall see him..." (Revelation 1:7)

You can only "be" to the degree that you see. The Lord made the Seeing Eye only to see how much good you can spot for yourself, or how much evil you choose to spot for yourself. Where are you in the picture of life? That is the story of your life.

Proverbs 22:9 says, *"He that hath a bountiful eye shall be blessed..."* If you do not have a bountiful eye, then you have a poverty eye. Not all healing happens instantly. That is not the normal process. There is a process to healing. A woman doesn't have a baby instantly; she must go through a process.

152

You must determine where you want your reality to be. Do you want your reality to be in real time or in God's time? Your disease will always get you back into real time. You will start seeing those numbers flashing at you saying, *"Look at what age you are and look at what you have not accomplished yet."*

> *"Be still, and know that I am God. I will be exalted among the nations; I will be exalted in the earth."* (Psalm 46:10)

Be still and be whatever you are recognizing at that moment. The Amplified Version reads, "Let be and be still, and know (recognize and understand) that I am God." Let be and be still. When something is not manifesting, there is something you're not recognizing and understanding. The Bible says, *"Get wisdom, and with all of thy getting get understanding."* Get an understanding. You can have wisdom, but you must know how to apply it for your thing. If you're chasing things, it means that you can't let be and be still. Sometimes God will keep you without just to see if you can let be and be still. However, anything you want to manifest just tap the invisible prophet within you.

VISITOR'S CARD

Bishop E. Bernard & Pastor Debra Jordan

Welcome you to

ZOE MINISTRIES!

(PLEASE PRINT)

First Name: _____ Last Name: _____

Address: _____

City: _____ State: _____ Zip Code: _____

Phone Day: ( ) _____ Eve: ( ) _____

E-Mail Address _____

How did you hear about us? (check) ☐ TV ☐ Friend

☐ Other: _____ Date of Birth _____

CHAPTER 10

THE INVISIBLE SUPPLY

— ✠ —

"Knowledge is power."

—Bishop E. Bernard Jordan

LOOK!

"Now there cried a certain woman of the wives of the sons of the prophets unto Elisha, saying, Thy servant my husband is dead; and thou knowest that thy servant did fear the Lord: and the creditor is come to take unto him my two sons to be bondmen. And Elisha said unto her, What shall I do for thee? tell me, what hast thou in the house? And she said, Thine handmaid hath not any thing in the house, save a pot of oil." (2 Kings 4:1-2)

What is in your hand? What is in your house? What you are looking for on the outside of you is already on the inside of you. Until you discover what is in your hand and what is in your house, you will walk in lack. For the Bible says, *"My people are destroyed for the lack of knowledge."* You only suffer lack because you don't know what is in your hand, and you don't know what is in your house. Until you know what is in your hand, you are poor.

This is a woman whose husband was one of the sons of the prophets, yet she did not know what was in her house, which shows us that because you sleep with a prophet does not make you a prophet. It also shows us that because you are a prophet, doesn't mean that you are going to be profitable. Every prophet is not profitable, because sometimes the prophet doesn't know what is in his hand or what is in his house.

When the woman went to the prophet he pointed her back to what was in her hand. The prophet is your invisible supply. Sometimes you may not understand why the prophet is in your life. The prophet is in your life to point you to the invisible supply that is trying to get to you. However, the invisible supply is going to come from something that is in your hand. What is in your hand? Until you get in touch with the supply you will not see the supply?

Sometimes you don't know what is in your house. You can be around a prophet and not realize that you are sitting in the midst of the prophet. You can be with the prophet and not even know that you are in touch with the invisible supply. You can walk with the supply and not know that you are with the supply because you lack knowledge of the supply.

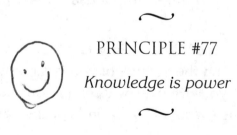

PRINCIPLE #77

Knowledge is power

The woman's sons were about to be sold off into slavery because they lacked knowledge of what was in their house, and they lacked the prophetic word that would tell them what to do with what was in their house. You are destroyed for the lack of knowledge. As long as you lack knowledge you will not receive the goods that are ordained for you.

> *"Then he said, Go, borrow thee vessels abroad of all thy neighbours, even empty vessels; borrow not a few. And when thou art come in, thou shall shut the door upon thee and upon thy sons, and shalt pour out into all of those vessels, and thou shalt set aside that which is full. (2 Kings 4:3-4)*

Miracles can only be worked behind the scenes. However, miracles will not begin to happen until you learn how to close the door. Start doing in secret so that God can bring your reward out in the open. When Jesus told His disciples to let down their nets, they had to get other people to help bring the miracle in. Jesus did not multiply the fishes and loaves. He needed someone else in the network, so He took the little boy's lunch, another one participating in the miracle. Show me a miracle in Scripture, and I will show you a hidden hand from a human level that had to be involved. God does not perform miracles without human intervention. God hides himself in a human element in order to bring forth the miracle that is created for your experience.

~

PRINCIPLE #78

Until you discover what is in your hand and what is in your house, you will walk in lack.

~

The only reason there is lack is in your life is because you don't know what is in your house. If you want to discover what is in your house, you have to go in your spiritual lab. *"Know ye not that ye are the temple."* Your body is the temple. The temple is your lab. Your body is the "template" of the living God. Going into your "lab" is like going into your imagination. When you go into your lab you may discover some areas of your life with which you are not satisfied, for example, your finances, family situations, relationships. But you must go within your imagination where creation begins and begin to change those facts into a desired result and develop a new image. Then you must keep the image in your mind.

> *Your future is created from seed that the Father has placed in your hand.*
>
> ~

It's In Your Hand

Everything begins with a seed. You were originally a seed, a white substance swimming around which happened to fertilize an egg. Millions of sperm were trying to get to that one egg, but you were the only one that made it, which means, you were the fittest. The universe only rewards and celebrates the fittest. Do not get involved with weak people. Weak people will make you weak. For those who are strong, weakness is your enemy.

Your future is created from seed that the Father has placed in your hand. Your harvest is created from seed that the Father has placed in your hand. "Elijah said unto the woman, *"What shall I do for thee?"* She came to the prophet with a complaint, and he pointed her back to an answer that was in her own house. *"Tell me, what has thou in the house?"* *"But you don't understand, they are about to take my son."* *"But what is in your house? What is in your hand?"* When you fail to work with what is in your hand you are not operating at your fullest potential. You are walking around in lack. However, it is time for you to shake yourself and get out of the place of lack, because the lack is in your own mindset.

> *"And it came to pass, when the vessels were full, that she said to her son, Bring me yet a vessel. And he said unto her, There is not a vessel more. And the oil stayed."* (2 Kings 4:6)

Notice, the oil kept pouring as long as there was a vacuum. Once there was no longer a vacuum to catch the oil, the oil ceased. For some people, your miracles have stopped because your "pot" was too small. When your vision is small, your oil will cease. If the place that you are in looks empty when you first obtain it, know that God will fill it shortly thereafter. God is not a waster. He will not cause your cup to run over if you don't have another cup to catch the overflow.

When Jesus multiplied the fishes and loaves, He allowed for there to be leftovers so that the disciples could pick up the fragments, as a sign, which caused the little boy to go back and tell his mother that Jesus took his lunch. The mother was upset for a moment because of the seed. However, the little boy said, "Wait a minute, Ma, before you pass out, look what Jesus did. He gave us groceries for a year!"

When God sends you the harvest and you are ready for it, He allows the harvest to go to the place where it can be settled. If you are not prepared, you will end up losing the harvest or wasting the overflow. Jesus told the fishermen to let down their nets. The fishermen, in unbelief, let down their nets and caught so many fish that the nets broke. (Luke 5:1-11) They lost all of the fish because they were not prepared for the harvest.

Sometimes God will stop sending you the harvest until you learn how to treat it. For some people, God is sending the harvest; however, they don't know what the harvest is. The harvest is staring them in the face, and they are staring the harvest in the face, but, they cannot discern it. They are looking for paper money, but God is saying, *"No, this is more valuable than any paper money you are going to get. You are going to be able to benefit from this for a whole lot more than what you can do with paper money."* It is important that you understand how to discern the harvest.

~

PRINCIPLE #79

God has created your promise through something that already exists in your life.

~

If God told you that He is going to make you wealthy, that is because there is something in your house that is going to create the wealth. You may say, "The prophet keeps prophesying to me about money and wealth, but I don't understand why I'm not seeing anything manifest." You don't know what is in your house. You need to see what is in your house, because your wealth is always in your house. Your wealth comes out of your present experience. Your wealth comes out of your present environment. Your wealth comes out of your present condition. Your wealth comes out of a present situation that you are unaware of because somehow you have been blinded in your mind's eye. Because you can't see the full picture of the wealth and prosperity that God has ordained for you, you walk in lack.

Your wealth has to be seen before it can be experienced.

Your wealth has to be seen before it can be experienced. Until you see it, you cannot be it. And if you don't be it, it is because you didn't see it. When you choose to see it, then you will be it. What I see is what I "be." What I see determines what I "be." If you can't see it, you will never be it.

"Say not ye, There are yet four months, and then cometh harvest?" (John 4:35) The professionals knew that factually the harvest was going to come in four months. They had already done the calculations. The woman with the issue of blood had gone to all the professionals, but they could do her no good. There comes a place where humanity cannot help. The only place you can get help from is from God. You can't understand it in your intellect because your intellect is saying, "Well, wait a minute, in four months." "Well, wait a minute, we fished all night. We are fisherman. You are a carpenter. Why are you going to tell us to let down our nets? We are going to just entertain you. Go ahead, let down a net, even though he said more than one net."

You have to get to a place where you can lift up your eyes and look on the fields.

161

The Father has placed a seed in your hand, and He is waiting for you to take that seed and give it. Your seed is what created your present experience. The lack of giving a seed is what has created the tragedy you are in. When you give the seed it creates the prosperity. Therefore, you want to check how your giving has been in the past, and look at your present. Your present is a result of a past seed that you sowed.

If you keep the seed to yourself, it is in the wrong pocket. What I keep I lose, and what I give I keep. The seed is like the two-edge sword. It will either bless you or curse you. It is either a seed or a weed. The seed has a two-fold purpose. If it is a seed it will grow something; if it is a weed, it is not in the right pot; therefore it will choke whatever is in the pot, because it doesn't belong there.

～

PRINCIPLE #80

Your harvest is created from the seed that
the Father has placed in your hand.

～

A weed is a seed in the wrong place. A weed can be a rose seed that is planted in an orange grove. Roses are beautiful when they are in their own arrangement. But if the rose seed gets over into an orange grove because somebody wanted to see roses and oranges grow together, the rose seed will start to choke out the orange seed because it doesn't belong in that environment. The orange seed contaminates the environment, and the seed is not able to grow properly.

The widow woman at Zarephath, was killing her son with her seed because she was putting her seed into the wrong pot. She kept putting the seed in her son's belly, but the seed belonged in the prophet's belly. When the seed went into the prophet's belly, the pot overflowed. What she thought was a seed was actually poisoning her son, killing him softly, because that pot was ordained for the prophet to feed out of. So she was planting the right seed, but planting it in the wrong pot.

Every seed is like a time capsule. It has a day to be born and a day to unfold. It will unfold whether it is in the right pot or not. When it is in the right pot it will be a harvest; when it is in the wrong pot it will be a weed choking out the good seed. It has a genetic code. For example, a prophet may tell you, "On February 25, your dream will be birthed. "Well, wait, I don't have a chance to get my offering to the prophet on the 25th, like I am supposed to. I was waiting for my next check on the 15th. So I am going to hold on to it because I have some things to do." So God says, "Be born anyway." Then you wonder and say, "My car was working perfect, and it just broke down. I wonder what's going on here." A seed was born, but you just had it in the wrong pot. You took the seed that you were supposed to sow to the prophet and paid your car note.

The reason you are in the situation that you are in is because you have a seed that is a good seed, but it is in the wrong environment, and the time capsule has broken. It is time for that thing to be born. That seed is looking for sunshine in New York, and you have it somewhere in California sitting. So it is just cracking your cement. And you wonder why the foundation of your house is coming apart. You have your seed in the wrong environment. When you have your seed growing in the wrong spot it will cripple your condition. A seed in the wrong area becomes a destructive force.

God never puts you in a situation where you are eternally in a dilemma. You have something in your house to give you a way out, but do you want to follow the instructions? Every seed has instructions. If a woman gets pregnant, that seed is supposed to be in the womb. If the seed gets trapped in the fallopian tube, it can be very painful. It can even kill the woman if she doesn't undergo an operation.

~

PRINCIPLE #81

Every seed has instructions.

~

Some people have money seed in their fallopian tubes. They are pregnant, but the seed is in the wrong environment. They know they have it, and they know it is growing. However, it will never bring them the right harvest because it landed in the wrong environment. Have you been putting your seed in the right area, or are you holding your seed? Where is your seed growing? The law of the seed is as long as the earth remaineth there will be seedtime and harvest. However, you don't want it growing in the wrong spot. All seed grows, but make sure it is not growing in the wrong place.

Give It To Me!

The widow woman at Zarephath had a seed in her pot that was killing her son, but she was being faithful. She didn't mean to poison her child, but she was poisoning him until the prophet came and showed her the invisible supply. The prophet said, "Put it in my belly." She replied, "But this is my last. We are going to eat and die." The woman knew she was killing her son. However, it was her last cake offering. The prophet had to come and say, "Hold it, stop. Give me the seed. Make me the cake first. I have to take the poison off of what you have. When you put the first fruit in the prophet's belly, you will see the harvest. You have it in the wrong belly."

When the prophet takes your seed and digests it, it comes out as a house that is paid for; it is a scholarship that is given; it is a blessing that grows and increases in a way that you cannot explain; it is a business that flourishes. The prophet is the invisible supply. The prophet comes to reveal the invisible supply, because it is there. The prophet never prophesies to your personality. It is not personal. The prophet only speaks to the principle. He does not speak unto condemnation. He does not cut to kill. He only cuts you to live. The prophet comes into your life as the invisible supply to show you how to access the supply.

Testimony Concerning the Seed

A woman came to one of my conferences and she made a pledge. However, when she made the pledge she had not received prior permission from her husband. She used her husband's credit card. The word of the Lord to her was that in the fullness of time she would bring forth a son, and that she would present the son to the prophet of God. She had a history of difficulty conceiving children. She tried to conceive for 15 years, with no success.

The husband didn't believe what the prophet said. So, he demanded that she pull back the pledge. However, after she pulled back the pledge she became pregnant, and in the fullness of time she was able to deliver a healthy baby. Unfortunately, two years later, the child died. Later she went to another prophet to inquire of the Lord regarding the death of her child. The prophet said to her, "You do not know what the man of God had to go through to bring forth your child into this realm. When the child took ill you should have taken the child and placed him at the feet of the prophet." Instead of taking the child to the hospital, the child was supposed to be taken to the prophet, because it wasn't a normal child. The child died because the covenant was broken.

When children come by supernatural pronouncement of a prophetic word, and trauma or drama happens to them, you cannot take them straight to the physician. You have to first take them to the prophet who prophesied their lives into existence. Oftentimes, people forget the source, the invisible supply.

Testimony Concerning the Seed

My wife received a prophetic word that she would give birth to a seventh child. When my wife was about seven months pregnant, we went to the doctor for her sonogram. The sonogram showed two brains. It looked like there were two "grapefruit-sized" brains. At that moment my wife began to panic. She said, "Should I get the amniocentesis?" I said, "No. You are pregnant because of the prophetic word." Then I said, "Well maybe we should abort the child." She said, "But you said…"

At that moment, I left my wife, ran to the bank and withdrew $2,000 from my account, which was all that I had. I drove a two-hour drive to the prophet's house and sat at his feet. I sowed the $2,000 seed and said, "This is the sonogram, and this is what the doctor said. The doctor said that this child is not going to live. She is going to be deformed, and she may not even make it." I said, "What do you say?" Bishop Jordan said, "It is just drama. The baby is going to live." Today, our daughter, Zoe, is four years old, and the only sign we have is a birthmark in the back of her neck as a sign of the prophetic word.

The prophet can tell you if the seed is not in the right place. When your pain becomes great enough you will listen to the prophet.

More Than Enough

"Let them shout for joy, and be glad, that favour my righteous cause: yea, let them say continually, Let the Lord be magnified, which hath pleasure in the prosperity of his servant." (Psalm35:27)

The Amplified says, *"Let those who favor my righteous cause and have pleasure in my uprightness shout for joy and be glad and say continually, Let the Lord be magnified, Who takes pleasure in the prosperity of his servants."* God takes pleasure in your prosperity. When you are not prosperous He has no pleasure.

In Matthew 25:15-26, one man was given two talents, another man five talents, and another man one. The men with the two talents and the five talents multiplied their talents. Their master said, *"Well done, thou good and faithful servant."* The man with the one talent took his money and put it away. He received no interest on it. The Bible called him a wicked servant, even though he gave back what he received just as he received it. However, his master perceived him as wicked because he never multiplied it. He never took a risk with what he was given. You are not faithful unless you are a multiplier. If you want to please God become a multiplier, become prosperous.

> *So, the prophet told the woman "Go sell the oil, and pay thy debt, and live thou, and the children of the rest."* (2 Kings 4)

You always have enough to create more. Until you believe that you have enough to create more, you will walk in lack. As long as you look outside of yourself for the blessing, the blessing will not come to you. Whatever enters your life will determine what will exit your life. When there is an entrance of some good in your life that means the papers are being handed out for the exit of something that has expired in your life. For example, when mortgage payments enter into your life, rental payments exit your life. When a vehicle enters your life, public transportation exits your life.

Until you believe that you have enough to create more, you will walk in lack.

Likewise, when God sends a blessing in your life expect some people to leave your life. There are some individuals in your life right now who will exit when the harvest comes.

So, get ready, because when God starts to send a harvest, He sends a hundredfold with persecution, because what enters your life is also going to create an exit. Never tell anyone, "We are going to be friends forever." There will be one harvest that will come into your life, and that friend will say, "No. This is just too much. I have to go."

There are things in your life right now that cannot remain in your life when the harvest comes, because it will choke the good seed. When the harvest comes the weeds must leave. God sends the harvest. God will not send a harvest from heaven until you let a seed leave earth. A seed must leave your hand before a harvest can come to you. You may say, "I want God to bless me." But what seed have you released. What seed did you sow? The seeds you sow will determine the harvest that will come to you.

If you bring your tithes into the storehouse, God said, *"I will open up the windows of heaven and pour you out a blessing that there is not room enough to receive."* (Malachi 3:10) Tithing is not a "subtracter." Tithing is a multiplier. Many people believe that when they give their tithes something is being subtracted from them. To the contrary, when you give your tithes, you are being multiplied. You sow the seed in faith, and God returns it back to you in the form of a harvest.

What is seed? Your seed is anything you have that could benefit and advance someone else. "God gives seed to the sower." Therefore, you should not hoard your seed. Also do not hoard your seed for the right opportunity to sow it, because when God gives you the seed, the right opportunity is before you to sow. Make sure that greed does not overtake you. Discern why God has sent the seed to you. The next time you have a hardship in your life, try to trace back what seed God told you to sow that you did not sow.

~

PRINCIPLE #82

Your seed controls your future.

~

There is a seed that is in your life right now that is designed to deliver you from some evil. However, if you don't sow it, it will create a tragedy. Your seed is the only thing that controls your future.

Seed is giving something to God with expectation. Never rob yourself of expectation, because even God looks for expectation. The Bible says, *"Whatsoever a man soweth, that shall he also reap."* (Galatians 6:7) The seed is giving something to God with the expectation that He will multiply it back where you need it the most. *"Give, and it shall be given unto you; good measure, pressed down, and shaken together, and running over, shall men give into your bosom. For with the same measure that ye mete withal it shall be measured again."* (Luke 6:38) Notice how it will be given to you, "good measure." Whatever you give will come back to you in a good measure. That is a guarantee.

Your faith brings the seed to you, and it takes faith to sow the seed for the harvest. Your seed produces the harvest. What is in your hand? What is in your house? What is within your reach? What is God calling you to sow that He chooses to grow? God multiplies your seed. He does not multiply your harvest. Your harvest is the finale; your seed is a beginning. So, if you eat your seed, you eat away the possibility of multiplication.

Many people eat the seed because they lack patience. Your seed is what God multiplies, and your faith is why God multiplies it. Provide the faith, and God will show you how He multiplies the seed. If there is no faith, there will be no multiplication. You always have enough to create more. Until you believe that you have enough to create more, you will walk in lack. As long as you look outside of yourself for the blessing, the blessing will not come to you.

~

PRINCIPLE #83

Your seed is the beginning, your harvest is the finale.

~

Whatever enters your life will determine what will exit your life. When there is an entrance of some good in your life, the papers are being handed out for the exit of something that has expired in your life. How much seed have you sowed into your flesh? There is a seed that is in your life right now that is designed to create a miracle. But there is also a seed that is in your life right now that, if left in your life, will create a tragedy. You have to sow it.

You will never be wealthy as long as you are looking for your wealth to be produced on the outside instead of from within you. If you are looking for a blessing, it means that you are without a blessing. It reveals that you are not a blessing. Check your temple. The prophet has to change what is in your mind before you can see the results in your hand.

The Raven

"And Elijah the Tishbite, who was of the inhabitants of Gilead, said unto Ahab, As the Lord God of Israel liveth, before whom I stand, there shall not be dew nor rain these years, but according to my word. And the word of the Lord came unto him, saying, "Get thee hence, and turn thee eastward, and hide thyself by the brook Cherith, that is before Jordan. And it shall be that thou shalt drink of the brook; and I have commanded the ravens to feed thee there." (1 Kings 17:1-4)

In 1 Kings 17:3, God told Elijah to "get by the Brook Cherith." In 17:4, he is told to drink by the brook. Notice, God commanded the raven to feed Elijah there. There is a mystery to the raven. The raven is known as an unclean bird. The raven is a blackbird, which denotes something that is unformed or dark.

Why would God send an unclean bird to a kosher prophet unless there was something that God wanted him to see? God is so awesome that He desires to get us out of the place of familiarity. As long as you are in your comfort zone, God cannot do anything in your life. It is almost like God's hands are tied. God wants to get you to the place where you don't know which way to go, that dark place, that place where you can't see your way, but yet you have to go there and begin to move around and function as God directs you. You are no longer leaning on your own understanding. You are no longer leaning on your own strength, but you are leaning on the strength of God.

It is in man's nature to be able to go to someone and ask for help. But God is raising up a people that will no longer reach out and say, "Help me," but who will begin to lift their hands up high unto the heavens from where their help comes. They are going to have a greater understanding that their help comes from the Lord God Almighty. They are going to understand that the silver is God's, the gold is God's, the cattle upon a thousand hills is God's. Everything that God made and created is on earth, and because you are in this earth realm it is yours. But you have to get to that place where you lean on nothing or no one, only God.

God is getting ready to take away the crutches. He is moving His people out of the place of familiarity. He is moving them out of their comfort zone. God is raising up a people, and He is telling them, "It is time to get out of your comfort zone. No longer will you lean on the left or the right, but you are going to lean totally on me." God will take you out to the desert, and you will think you're dying, but God says, "I am giving you a resurrection." It's time to stop looking for help from here and there and begin to know in whom you believe. If we say we serve God who is all in all, then let's begin to demonstrate it.

~

PRINCIPLE #84

God is all in all.

~

Sometimes God will send that which is without form into your life to sustain you. I believe God is trying to see what we will do and how we will react. Are we afraid of the darkness? Many people don't want to go into the dark place. They would rather have the lights on. The darkness is too cumbersome. It surrounds them. It engulfs them. They can't handle the darkness. But it is in the darkness where we begin to form our unformed purposes. God is saying, "Fear not. Go in the dark and form it because it is already in you. It is already a part of you. I am looking for you to just speak it into being." God wants you to trust Him in the dark. It is that complete and overall trust that He is looking for from us, and then He can lead us into the abundant life. But as long as we are afraid of the darkness, we won't get all that God has for us.

Sometimes God will send that which is without form into your life to sustain you.

Sometimes God will send that which is without form into your life to sustain you. The raven shows up in your life at different seasons just to see if you are going to say, *"Well, I don't want to deal with that."* You can discern that it is God sending you a "raven experience," which is something that is unformed, or someone who has shifted in his shape, or something that is unrecognizable to the natural mind or to the intellect.

Isn't it interesting that God caused the prophet to be sustained by something that was dark, something that was unclean, something that was hidden, something that symbolizes the unformed. What is God saying to us in this hour? You have to get ready to know how to master your unformed purposes. The prophet is in your life to open up your vision to see not only your future, but your present. Sometimes there is a treasure hidden in the dark but unless you are open to searching out the matter, you will remain ignorant of the blessing. That is why the prophet comes to point you to your invisible supply. Sometimes you have to let be, and then the word will manifest itself as being.

~

PRINCIPLE #85

The prophet is your invisible supply.

~

The Prophet's Offering

"He that receiveth a prophet in the name of a prophet shall receive the prophet's reward; and he that receiveth a righteous man in the name of a righteous man shall receive a righteous man's reward." (Matthew 10:41)

The widow woman at Zarephath could not receive her miracle until she came in contact with the prophet. How you treat the prophet of God in your midst will determine your blessing. Have you received the prophet's reward? There was a woman who built a chamber for the man of God. Then the man of God came to her and asked, "What do you need? Do you need to be known of men?" There is a level of the prophetic where the prophet can decree something which may not necessarily be the Word of the Lord, but may be your reward. Elijah asked Elisha, "What do you want?" There is a gift or a service that can be rendered that can provoke the prophet to say, "What do you want?"

175

~

PRINCIPLE #86

*How you treat the prophet of God will
determine your blessing.*

~

Poor people do not think generationally. They only think for the present, the immediate "now." However, wealth is a mindset. Wealthy people plan for future generations. They will see a religious institution and say, *"I must keep this alive in the earth, so I am going to take out a policy for a million dollars and leave it to this ministry, so that my children and my children's children will have a place to feed."* When we depart the earth we should leave a gift that yet speaketh. What will you leave behind after you go home to be with the Lord? Where is your gift that yet speaketh?

Obedience produces miracles. There is a blessing that comes with the obedience of giving the offering in a specified manner and at a specified time. In Scripture, whenever a person gave an offering of obedience he received a blessing. Giving is not measured by how much you give, but it is measured by how much you have left over after you give. Jesus sat over the treasury and watched what the people were giving. That is how He knew that the widow had given her last. There were many rich people giving in the temple, however, the widow gave more than them all. She gave all of her living. Never become concerned about the amount of your offering. A thousand dollars to one person might be a widow's mite to someone else. There are some large offerings that are given in disobedience that God will not smile upon.

However, secret giving is only appropriate when you give to the poor. A religious mindset says, "I am not into offering lines and asking people to stand and declare what they are going to give. I think that should be done in secret." However, the Bible says that you should give alms to the poor in secret." (Matthew 6:1-4)

A blessing can actually be considered a reward. When you give to the prophet you will receive the prophet's reward. However, you must understand how to meet the prophet.

Many people do not understand how to meet the prophet. They get the prophet's word; however, they do not see the reward. Could there be some prophetic words hanging in the air that have not come to pass because you have not made a deposit into the prophet's life?

You may think that it is not necessary to give to a prophet, that the prophet should give the prophetic without thought of compensation. Many people say, "After all, it's the Word of the Lord, and Jesus said, freely have you received, freely give." However, there is a big difference between the words "free" and "freely." People pay large sums of money to receive legal counsel or medical counsel. The church is the only institution on earth that wants to deny the laborer his wages. We want the man of God to see for us, and pray for us, but we don't want him fed. We will draw from his cistern, but we will not make a deposit. Think of the number of people in the church who may be faithful in giving to the church, but will not give to the man of God. The widow woman at Zarephath did not give to Elijah's ministry, but she gave to his belly. What she sowed in the prophet's belly determined what came into her mouth.

∼

PRINCIPLE #87

Obedience produces miracles.

∼

The Reverse

God used an unclean creature to sustain a "kosher" prophet. He was not supposed to eat from the raven. However, in this hour God is bringing the wealth of the wicked into the hands of the righteous. He is using unclean things to sustain the prophet. Many people do not understand the fullness of truth concerning people receiving salvation. The Bible speaks of some people who had to give an offering in order to receive salvation. The rich young ruler asked Jesus, *"What must I do to have eternal life?"* However, he kept the commandments from his youth, and he was morally good. It is interesting that Jesus never said, *"Repent of your sins and confess Me as your Lord and Savior."* Jesus answered the young ruler by saying, *"Sell all that you have and give to the poor."* Zachias wanted salvation, so he had to go out and start giving in order to enter the kingdom.

Many people have received salvation into the kingdom of God whether they were drug dealers, Mafia, etc. However, we should make private appointments with them and say, "You have caused so much damage in the kingdom that you must give "x" amount." Absolution demands an offering. In observing the Catholic rulership, when a particular Philippine leader's wife desired absolution, she had to bring an offering before forgiveness was extended to her. Many people in our churches today do not understand this concept.

Many people think money is unspiritual and that it has nothing to do with God and the kingdom. Most people subconsciously think that money is dirty. However, money is a spiritual force. The hands that handle it determine whether it is righteous or unrighteous.

Jesus' lifestyle was quite elegant. The people cast lots for His garments. When He was ready to go to Jerusalem, He didn't want a used car, but he said, "Get me an ass which a man never sat on." He told a thief to hold the money bag. You don't have a treasurer unless you have an excess of money. Jesus did not disciple poor people. He preached the gospel to the poor, but he discipled the rich. Notice, when Jesus performed miracles, the recipients said, *"Jesus, we want to follow you."* Jesus said, *"No. Go and start your public ministry. Go tell the testimony. I don't need for you to follow me right now."* However, when someone rich came into His presence, He said, *"Come and follow me. I will make you..."*

~

PRINCIPLE #88

God is bringing the wealth of the wicked into the hands of the righteous.

~

Poor people are not discipleship material. The problem with some of our churches today is that we have preachers in the pulpit who are poor. Poor people look for immediate gratification. A person who is too hungry will devour anything, including you. There are some people who are grieved over

179

money. However, they are grieved only because they don't have money, but money has them.

> *"And Jesus looked round about, and saith unto his disciples, How hardly shall they that have riches enter into the kingdom of God! And the disciples were astonished at his words."* (Mark 10:23-24)

Some people may interpret this scripture as saying rich people cannot enter the kingdom. However, upon further examination we see what Jesus was really saying. *"But Jesus answereth again, and saith unto them, Children, how hard is it for them that trust in riches to enter into the kingdom of God!"* (Mark 10:24)

There are individuals who will not enter the kingdom because of their trust in riches. Tithing is the minimum that a person is required to do. You are not blessed for tithing. As a matter of fact, tithing opens the windows of heaven, and the offering determines how the blessings will flow. Therefore, giving actually starts at 11%. This is the outer court revelation. According to the scripture, Israel seemed to have given three tithes. That is why God said, "You have robbed me in tithes and offerings."

~

PRINCIPLE #89

When you give to the prophet you will receive the prophet's reward.

~

The reason there is no meat in your house of worship is because the people are not really tithing. Nothing is in the storehouse because the man of God has not been given enough substance to stay in the presence of God and bake the meat of revelation that the house needs. When you bring the tithes, God says, "Prove me now." God wants to open you, oh, windows of heaven, and then He wants to pour you out. He wants to fill you with ideas and "pour you out." A Hebrew commentary interprets this as, "I want to pour you out a blessing that your mouth will get tired of saying, "Enough! Enough! Enough!"

"It is easier for a camel to go through the eye of the needle." (Mark 10:25)

The eye of the needle was a gate going into Jerusalem. In order for the camel to go through the eye of the needle, he had to unload all of the baggage and go through naked. However, he would pick up the baggage on the other side. The camel was willing to unload in order to get through the gate and into the city. However, many people have to pray before unloading a hundred dollars or a thousand dollars. A camel doesn't pray about unloading. The camel just unloads and goes through, because he picks it all up on the other side.

"And they were astonished out of measure, saying among themselves, Who then can be saved? And Jesus looking upon them saith, With men it is impossible, but not with God: for with God all things are possible. Then Peter began to say unto him, Lo, we have left all, and have followed thee. And Jesus answered and said, Verily I say unto you, There is no man that hath left house, or brethren, or sisters, or father, or mother, or wife, or children, or lands, for my

sake, and the gospel's. But he shall receive an hun-dred-fold now in this time, houses, and brethren, and sisters, and mothers, and children, and lands, with persecutions; and in the world to come eternal life."
(Mark 10:26-30)

You cannot receive the hundredfold unless you unload. The hundredfold brings persecution. When you start preaching wealth and prosperity, you will have persecution.

The widow woman was commanded by God, yet she didn't know it. In the same way, some of you are command-ed by God, but you don't know it. She was preparing for death. Likewise, some of you are prepared for death. You are crying, "My job is folding up, and my company is leav-ing. I don't know what I am going to do." And then God sends you a prophet.

God could have sent Elijah to somebody who was rich, someone who could have given out of their abundance. But whenever God gets ready to bless someone through a prophet, He sends someone in the prophet's life with a greater need. God creates a need in the prophet's life just to give you an opportunity to fill it.

∼

PRINCIPLE #90

*God dries the brook in the prophet's life
to get a miracle into your life.*

∼

Who you are called to sustain determines how you are maintained. Until you unlock the vision of your man of God, your vision will never be unlocked. Some people have their leaders living in homes that are stressful. You have them driving vehicles where they have to pray down the road going from one meeting to the next. However, God is disturbed and grieved by how you have treated His servant.

So God is saying, *"I will hold up your houses, and I will hold up your blessing. I will even close doors and not allow contracts to get signed that you are believing God to be signed. Because you have withheld your substance from the man of God, I am withholding My substance from you."*

The widow woman had to give to the man of God first, then he told her what would happen. So, she went and did according to the saying of Elijah. Paul says, "If any man comes to preach any other gospel which I did not preach, let him be accursed." (Galatians. 1:8) In other words, if you did not hear it from me, it is not God. The widow woman didn't say to Elijah, "Let me pray about it and see if it is God."

> *Remember, miracles can only take place through a human element.*
> ~

Sheep cannot make decisions. Sheep must be led or else they will go astray. Many people have gone astray in their giving because they have refused to be led by a shepherd. However, you will not be able to cross your "Red Sea" until you locate the hand that is called to part your "sea." Whenever God begins to part your waters He will use the hand of a man. Remember, miracles can only take place through a human element. It is an insult to go to the man of God empty handed. You can be right in Spirit, but wrong in principle.

Saul replied, "If I don't have a present, I cannot go into the man of God's presence." Israel could not appear before the Lord empty-handed. Many people are like spiritual eunuchs. They do not deserve to hear the word because they refuse to produce a seed.

You are at the brink of seeing fulfillment in your life. There are levels that God wants to bring you to, but He wants you to exercise your faith by sowing the seed so that He can work a miracle in your life. The widow woman of Zarephath could have chosen to disobey the prophet and eat her last cake by herself. However, she understood that her miracle was dependent upon her obedience and her trust in the man of God. Who are you trusting today?

∽

PRINCIPLE #91

Giving starts at 11%.

∽

APPENDIX

PROPHETIC AFFIRMATION

I am able to do exceedingly, abundantly, above all that I can ask or think, according to the power that worketh in me. Thank you, Holy Spirit. We honor You today. We honor Your Presence among us. We honor Your work among us. Move among us today. Shine on us today. Be God in us today. Amen

OTHER BOOKS BY BISHOP E. BERNARD JORDAN

Achiever's Guide to Success

Breaking Soul Ties and Generational Curses

His Color Was Black: A Race Attack

Cosmic Economics

Cosmic Economics: The Universal Keys to Wealth Workbook

The Holy Spirit

"I AM" Mar Elijah the Root: Teaching on the Laws of the Spirit

The Joshua Generation

Keys to Liberation

The Making of the Dream

The Marital Union of Thought

The Mastery of Mentorship

Meditation: A Key to New Horizons in God

Mentoring: An Iconoclastic Approach to the Development of Ministry

Mentoring—The Missing Link

The Power of the Dime

The Power of Money

Praise & Worship

Prayer of Fasting

Prophetic Congress: Deep Calleth Upon Deep

Prophetic Congress: Deep Calleth Upon Deep *workbook*

Prophetic Congress "The Summit" Volume I)—Out of Print

Prophetic Congress "The Summit" Volume II)

Prophetic Genesis
The School of the Prophets Volume I—
The School of the Prophets Volume II Hardcover
The School of the Prophets Volume II
The Science of Prophecy
The Science of Prophetic Leadership
The Seed of Destiny
Servanthood
The Spirit of Liberation
The Spirit of the Oppressor
Spiritual Protocol: A Supplement to, Mentoring—The Missing Link
Unveiling the Mysteries
What Every Woman Should Know About Men
Written Judgments Volume 1
Written Judgments Volume 2
Written Judgments Volume 3
Written Judgments Volume 4

Minibooks
Above All Things Get Wisdom
Calling Forth the Men of Valor
The Purpose of Tongues

FREE WRITTEN PROPHECY

As seen on TV!

To get your free personal written word in the mail from me, Master Prophet E. Bernard Jordan simply visit our site at www.bishopjordan.com and follow the prompts. The Master Prophet will see the Mind of God on your behalf and he will give you the ANSWERS YOU HAVE BEEN SEEKING.